MONEY MATTERS

MATTERS

for *Newlyweds*

LARRY BURKETT

JANET
THOMA
BOOK

THOMAS NELSON PUBLISHERS®
Nashville

A Division of Thomas Nelson, Inc.
www.ThomasNelson.com

Published in Nashville, Tennessee, by Thomas Nelson, Inc.

Scripture taken from the NEW AMERICAN STANDARD BIBLE®, Copyright The Lockman Foundation 1960, 1962, 1963, 1968, 1971, 1972, 1973, 1975, 1995. Used by permission. (www.Lockman.org)

Library of Congress Cataloging-in-Publication Data

Burkett, Larry.
    Money matters for newlyweds / Larry Burkett.
        p. cm.
    ISBN 0-7852-6480-9
    1. Married people—Finance, Personal. 2. Finance, Personal.
3. Finance, Personal—Religious aspects—Christianity. I. Title.
    HG179 .B83856 2002
    332.024'0655—dc21   2002003688

Printed in the United States of America
02 03 04 05 06 BVG 5 4 3 2 1

CONTENTS

INTRODUCTION

Welcome to marriage! I would like to thank you for choosing to read this book. Essentially, it's made up of questions I've been asked by engaged and newlywed couples over the last fifteen years, on our daily *Money Matters* radio program. During this time, I think I've heard basically every question on money that can be asked—from a biblical perspective.

To the best of my ability, I've tried to answer these questions honestly and, when possible, to quote the Scripture that deals with the specific question. As you might imagine, in most instances my answers are based on my limited knowledge of some complicated economic issues presented in a short, to-the-point manner. Therefore, as you read this book you'll often see the phrase "in my opinion," and it means exactly that.

Shortly after I became a Christian, as I read through the Bible in my personal study time, one of the things that greatly impressed me was how many Scriptures there are that deal with the area of money. Because of my educational background, I was attracted to the wisdom and simplicity of what the Bible had to say about money management. Over one year, I spent my spare time organizing those Scriptures that dealt with money. Usually what I would do in my own devotion time was ask myself questions like, "Okay, what does the Bible say about borrowing?" Then I would review all the Scriptures dealing with money, looking for those that dealt specifically with borrowing. I would highlight them and label those Scriptures "borrowing."

Without realizing it, I had started a topical concordance of finances. I still have the three notebooks that I compiled those many years ago, and I still use them in my study. They outline God's principles of handling money, and they form the foundation for all the answers I give in my books and on my radio program on the subject of money.

Through the years, I have had the opportunity to share these principles with thousands of couples, but I can still remember being amazed by the first couple I ever counseled. They were making about twice as much as I was at that time, and yet they were deeply in debt. Back then, a large amount of debt would have been $2,000 in credit cards, and this couple owed about $10,000. Clearly, they made a significant amount of money—more than enough to be able to manage it well and stay out of debt—and yet they were going further into debt every month.

As I talked to them, I realized several things. These habits had been developed over a long period of time. They both had come from fairly wealthy families, but they had no concept of how to handle money. I also realized that whatever I could talk them into somebody else could talk them out of. In other words, no matter what I said, someone selling a new boat, car, or swimming pool could turn them in that direction.

So I shared with them some of the biblical principles about money that I had been studying from the book of Proverbs. In fact, during the time I was counseling them (probably the better part of six months), I outlined a short Bible study for them that dealt with their debt problems. Actually, debt was not their real problem; debt was only a symptom. Their problems were poor training and indulgence.

I have become increasingly convinced of the importance of financial guidelines in marriage—from the very beginning of the journey together. Much of the debt and heartache associated with money woes could be avoided if couples became more knowledgeable and incorporated that knowledge.

In our society debt is a plague. It is the number one tool that Satan is using to destroy families and to disenfranchise Christians—literally, to defeat them. That's true at all ages—all the way down to the teenage years now, because young people are being saddled with more and more debt. Most young couples today tell me that debt is the number one problem they have. Current statistics tell us that about one-half of all new marriages (first marriages) are going to dissolve within the first six years.

About 80 percent of those couples who are divorced also say that most of the problems they had were financial. It's my opinion that they weren't having financial problems; they were having financial *symptoms*. The real problem probably was ignorance, indulgence, or a whole variety of other issues. The symptom was the debt that built up. It's time we really took this in hand and tried to solve the problems that manifest themselves in the form of debt.

What I found when I was counseling couples was that God seldom, if ever, puts similar people together in a marriage. If He did, one would be unnecessary. Opposites normally attract. So usually one spouse will be a spender and one will be a saver. One will be a worrier and the other will seem to never have a care. One will get up late and the other early. One will be sloppy and the other neat. And it goes on and on.

By putting opposites together, God makes one whole person, which is exactly what His Word says in the Old Testament: *"For this reason a man shall leave his father and his mother, and be joined to his wife; and they shall become one flesh"* (Genesis 2:24).

One person. But because people are opposites, they're going to approach their problems differently. One spouse is going to be worried and want to deal with the problem, but the other one won't want to be bothered and may want to just ignore it. I would say, more often than not, it's the wife who is concerned with the situation and wants to solve it. The husband may be concerned about it, but he just wants to avoid the issue.

Then there are the husbands who are more than willing to deal with problems, as long as it doesn't cost them anything. But you know what? If you're making payments on a bass boat and that's keeping you from being able to balance your budget, the bass boat (or whatever) has to go. But again, remember that opposites do attract and what may frighten one may not bother the other. You don't want to give up because you don't agree. Keep in mind that you are opposites and don't overreact.

Most important, keep in mind it takes two people to work on problems. No one person can be stuck with this burden and expect the problems to go away. Both husband and wife must work together. And remember, in general (and this is a broad generalization), many women worry too much, and many men spend too much.

I found in my counseling that although, in large part, people categorize women as the spenders, many times that's not true. Under impulse, women will often spend too much on food and clothes. Under the same impulse, the husband will go out and buy a new boat, a motor home, or an airplane. We men may not spend as often, but when we do we buy big-ticket items, and we tend to get very attached to them.

I trust this book will be a first step in answering the questions you have. You will find that most of the questions I have chosen to include are from first-time newlyweds, dealing with the "typical" first-time newlyweds' financial issues. I pray this book will encourage and bless you as you begin an exciting lifetime together.

1

COMMUNICATION

*A*s you begin your marriage, you will discover communication is essential in every area of your relationship, and financial matters are no exception. Money and its associated problems do not necessarily cause poor communication in a marriage, but they certainly reveal it. Most of our daily lives revolve around money—including making it, spending it, saving it, giving it, and the like.

It has been said that 80 percent of our lives is spent in the accumulation and distribution of money, so it's little wonder that the lack of communication will be reflected in money as well.

Many couples talk *at* each other about money, but few really talk about money in a way that allows both to voice their true feelings. Most couples are opposites (they really *do* attract) and, as such, each brings a different set of wants and needs to the table. The couple who learns to use money as a tool for communication learns a lot about each other and about balance.

Money is a great area in which to learn how to communicate,

because it is objective and measurable. Use it wisely, and your relationship will grow stronger. Ignore it, and perhaps you'll find yourself starting over again with somebody new, who may be remarkably like the previous spouse.

God's plan is that your marriage should prosper and grow, and money can help.

QUESTION:

Should we rent or buy?

My fiancée and I are getting married soon and we're getting a lot of conflicting advice. My parents tell me that it's foolish to waste money on rent and get no return. Unfortunately, most of the homes that we've looked at are beyond our financial capability. My fiancée's father is willing to lend us a down payment and make the monthly payments for the first year if we want to buy a nice home. It sounds very appealing to me, but I wonder if it is the right thing to do.

ANSWER:

There are two factors to consider about buying or renting. The first is what your budget allows. The second is whether it's the right decision for *you*.

If you have the money to make a down payment and you can afford the monthly payments, it may be a good financial decision to buy. However, I usually advise young couples not to buy in the first year of their marriage. There's enough stress on your life, just getting to know each other, without adding any additional stress.

If you let someone loan you the down payment and assume a monthly payment larger than what you can afford, you're taking on a contingent liability. Scripturally, what you're doing is taking on surety: an obligation to pay without a certain way to pay it.

Even though I appreciate the concern of your parents, remember that you and your fiancée are adults, and you need to make these decisions yourselves. The number one cause of financial problems with many young couples is that they buy a home that's too expensive for them. And although your father-in-law said that he would make the monthly payments for the first year, let me assure you: That year will pass very quickly and then you'll be stuck with making the payments. What happens after the first year if you can't afford those payments?

Bear in mind this simple proverb: *"Prepare your work outside, and make it ready for yourself in the field; afterwards, then, build your house"* (Proverbs 24:27). I think that's very good wisdom. In other words, get your life squared away, settle into a comfortable routine, live on a balanced budget, and then think about buying a home. And be sure it's a home that's within your means.

In your situation, I recommend that you relax for a year, get to know each other, and then think about buying a home.

QUESTION:
How can I tell my husband about the debt I brought into our marriage, which I've been keeping a secret?

I've always had bad credit, and after listening to your radio program I realized I have dishonored my husband. When we married, over a year ago, I decided not to tell him about my debt, which resulted from my misuse of credit cards. I have been juggling my finances, trying to keep this quiet, but I don't want to do this anymore.

ANSWER:

The best way to tell him is to be totally honest. Show him exactly what you owe and ask for his forgiveness for not being honest with him. He married you, he is your husband, you are both one, and your responsibilities are his responsibilities.

Obviously this can be a tough lesson, but it also can be a positive experience in your marriage. He may get a bit irritated when you confess, but let me assure you that most husbands appreciate honesty.

"He who walks in integrity walks securely, but he who perverts his ways will be found out" (Proverbs 10:9).

QUESTION:

Even though I want to be a good wife, and I know that the Bible says that my husband is the authority in the home, shouldn't I have some input in this marriage as well?

My husband acts more like a dictator than a leader in our home. He's chosen to manage all our finances, even though I believe that I'm a better bookkeeper than he is. I have absolutely no say over anything about finances: He buys our food, pays the bills, and even selects my clothes.

ANSWER:

Yes, you should have input in the marriage. God directs a husband to give his family balanced, godly leadership—not establish a dictatorship. A husband who wants to be a godly leader should take Jesus as his example. Jesus was a gentle leader. He never crushed somebody else's spirit to assert His authority.

The apostle Paul said, *"The husband is the head of the wife, as*

Christ also is the head of the church" (Ephesians 5:23). But he also said, *"Husbands, love your wives, just as Christ also loved the church"* (Ephesians 5:25). And, *"Be imitators of God, as beloved children; and walk in love, just as Christ also loved you, and gave Himself up for us"* (Ephesians 5:1–2).

A marriage between two people is much like the relationship between a right hand and a left hand: They are well matched but opposites. The key to a good partnership is to determine each other's assets and liabilities and then work together in love (no dictator needed).

It helps to remember that to have authority doesn't mean to be a ruler. Authority implies responsibility. Being a good authority figure means being a strong enough person not to be threatened by somebody else's strengths, particularly a spouse's.

The Bible tells husbands to love their wives and treat them as partners—literally coheirs: *"You husbands . . . live with your wives in an understanding way, as with a weaker vessel, since she is a woman; and grant her honor as a fellow heir of the grace of life"* (1 Peter 3:7).

Acting as a dictator is a sure sign of being insecure. Try not to take it personally. Your husband is an insecure person and you need to get to the source of it. Ask him to go for counseling, and if he won't go you need to pray about it—but don't badger him. *"The way of a fool is right in his own eyes, but a wise man is he who listens to counsel"* (Proverbs 12:15).

Even though the apostle Paul said that wives were to be subject to their husbands, that doesn't make you a nonperson in your home. You are to be your husband's helpmate, and one responsibility that any wife has is to help her husband make godly decisions.

My counsel is to share honestly with your husband how you feel. If you can't say it verbally, write it down for him, and then offer some alternatives. He may not even be aware of how important it is to you to be making some of the decisions or at least to be involved in the decision process. You might consider saying (or writing) something like this: "I believe that God has created me to be your helpmate. I love you and I would like to help by handling the budget for our household items, at least the ones that affect the home." Try to find some common ground on which you both can agree.

If, after sharing your feelings, your husband doesn't respond, go to your pastor, describe the problem, and see if he can help. Both you and your husband would need to attend this counseling, because he has to understand how you really feel.

QUESTION:

Is it taking authority away from the husband if the wife is the primary wage earner while the husband attends school?

My fiancé is in school, and we're getting married next year. I'm wondering if it would be proper for me to support us while he is in school?

ANSWER:

The two of you need to discuss this issue very honestly. Also, ask yourself if you are willing to work, without any bitterness or resentment, while he goes to school. Do you want to do it? Will it bother you that your husband isn't working? What will happen if you decide to go back to school, or what if you get pregnant? Can he accept that? Would he be willing to drop out of school if necessary? These are all questions you both need to answer honestly.

Personally, I can see nothing wrong with the wife working while her husband is in school, as long as you don't have any children. The apostle Paul says, *"If anyone does not provide for his own, and especially for those of his household, he has denied the faith, and is worse than an unbeliever"* (1 Timothy 5:8). That doesn't mean you can't work while he's in school, but it does mean that over the long-term the husband is to be the provider.

I have real concerns for any couple when the wife immediately goes to work to support them. She can easily become resentful. I've seen it many, many times, particularly if she doesn't want to be the sole provider. I've also noted that sometimes it makes the husband feel very inadequate.

I've known of situations in which the wife worked and the marriages were fine—they didn't have a problem—but I've also seen marriages dissolve because of the role conflicts that were caused. That's just as true when the husband was in seminary and the wife was working full-time.

So be very careful. Pray about it before you make your decision.

QUESTION:

Do you think that God can use a woman to head the household if her husband is weak-willed?

I've heard you talk many times about the wife supporting her husband and allowing him to be head of the home. However, I know that I am a better leader in many ways than my husband is. He leaves the cars without gas, is disorganized, and never questions a price or challenges any salesperson. I call around checking on home insurance costs and trying to get the best buy

I can; my husband won't do that because our agent is a friend from church.

ANSWER:

As I've said so often: God never puts two similar people together, because if He did one of them is unnecessary. One of you is going to be a leader and the other is going to be a follower. Sometimes that's the husband, sometimes it's the wife.

The husband's authority is established in God's Word: *"Encourage the young women to love their husbands, to love their children . . . being subject to their own husbands, that the word of God may not be dishonored"* (Titus 2:4–5).

No, I do not believe that you should usurp his authority. Even though he may not have your willpower, he still has God's authority, and God is going to bless your husband. You should work with him, support him, help him to make these decisions, and point out, when necessary, that maybe he didn't get the best buy or make the best decision. But do this in a nonaccusatory manner. That's the role of the supporter. "Not fair," you say? I agree, but it still doesn't change God's Word.

It would be no different from a good general who had a colonel under his authority who was the better military adviser. Napoleon Bonaparte was probably the best example of this. He was a brilliant strategist, but he was not an implementor. After Napoleon's brilliant motivating speeches were over and the battle plans were drawn up, it was the colonel who drew the plans and directed the troops, because Napoleon knew his own strengths and weaknesses.

The same principle is true in your situation. You may be a better manager and organizer and have a more forceful personality, but your role as a wife is to be a helpmate for your husband. Don't undermine his authority; build it up. And every chance you get, rather than telling people how much better you are at managing the household than he is, tell them how much you depend on him and what a godly man he is.

QUESTION:

Do you think two people from vastly different financial backgrounds can make a go of marriage?

I'm from a family of modest income and we managed our money very closely. My fiancée is from a very affluent home and her father's annual income is the equivalent of ten years of my father's income. It has caused some problems already, because the restaurants I want to go to she considers to be beneath her. Also, I know what kind of a honeymoon we can afford, and her expectations are at least ten times greater than mine. Her father is willing to pay for it, but I still wonder if this will cause a problem after we're married. Do you believe that these differences are so great that we shouldn't get married?

ANSWER:

Different financial backgrounds can have an enormous impact on a marriage, but different backgrounds don't always dictate a failed marriage. Interestingly enough, the spouse from the wealthy background isn't always the spender—any more than the spouse from a poor background is always a saver. Often the opposite is true.

If your fiancée's family, even though wealthy, managed their money wisely, then she may become a prudent money handler. However, you do need to discuss this very honestly *before* you get married.

I recommend you read *Money in Marriage* (see page 122), because it will help you understand each other: your goals, your aspirations, and how you think about money. Although you come from a lower-income family, it's great that your father and mother helped you learn how to manage money properly.

Very often, though, people from poorer families may feel that they did without while growing up, so now that they're out on their own they're going to live it up; so you need to watch for that as well.

A successful marriage depends on your backgrounds, your training, your personalities, and, most of all, your commitment to the Lord. The most important thing is that you understand each other, know what your goals are, discuss them thoroughly, and see if you can work out these things before you're married. Let me assure you, if you can't work it out before you're married, it won't get any easier once you are married. If you can't agree, you probably do need to postpone your marriage.

Many couples think that because they are Christians they will always be able to work out their problems later. Sadly, Christians get divorced as often as non-Christians do and over the same issues—generally money problems. *"The prudent sees the evil and hides himself, but the naive go on, and are punished for it"* (Proverbs 22:3). So you don't want to go into a marriage without facing a possible problem.

QUESTION:

What can I do about a fiancée who won't discuss financial matters?

I'm twenty-eight and engaged to a twenty-four-year-old Christian woman from a very fine family, but she is totally unwilling to discuss anything financial. I believe that God has called me to the mission field, and I know that I'm not going to make a lot of money. I need to know exactly how my fiancée feels about this, but her parents never talked about money in her home and she won't either. Her father handled all the money and her mother never even knew how much he made or where it was spent. I am in a quandary. I love her, but I don't know what to do.

ANSWER:

In my opinion you should delay your marriage until you and your fiancée can discuss your finances. You should be very honest with her about your plans for the mission field, and find out how she feels about it. Initially, many young couples say, "Well, God will just provide for us." That's true, but the Bible also says, *"The mind of man plans his way, but the LORD directs his steps"* (Proverbs 16:9).

We're to be a part of God's plan, not just observers of it. If you marry with these uncertainties about your wife's feelings, you may find out too late that she resents your career path and the tight money that's going to accompany it. It is going to be a difficult life at best, and unless you are both absolutely committed it very possibly won't work out.

Don't think that this will get easier once you're married. On the contrary, it will become more difficult. I recommend that the two of you go through our workbook, *Money in Marriage* (see page 122).

If you find that she isn't willing to do this, go to her pastor and explain your problem to him. Perhaps he can talk to the two of you together.

If you can't work this out, cancel the marriage plans. Otherwise, you're courting disaster.

QUESTION:

Is keeping the records and paying the bills always the husband's responsibility, or can it be the wife's?

We've been married for a few months and I've been keeping our home financial records because I have more time to do it than my husband, and I believe that I'm more detailed. But I heard a Christian teacher recently say that all these kinds of things should be the husband's responsibility.

ANSWER:

If a wife has the ability to manage the home finances, there's absolutely nothing unscriptural about her doing so, as long as she and her husband work together. They should both develop and maintain the budget—in other words, they both have a part in it. Then the wife can keep the records, but she and her husband should make the decisions together.

It's important, though, that the husband be in control if there are financial problems. That's especially true with delinquent bills. The husband should take charge and work out the arrangements with the creditors. As the biblical authority in the home, the husband should bear the emotional pressure of creditor harassment. Remember what Ephesians 5:25 says: *"Husbands, love your wives, just as Christ also loved the church and gave Himself up for her."*

In the final analysis, if you're the better bookkeeper and paying the bills doesn't create a rift in the marriage, I say go for it. That's why God gave you the gifts you have.

QUESTION:

Is it a good idea to leave money to my wife in a trust, so she can spend the income but not the principal during her lifetime?

Even though we're both in our late-twenties, I like to plan for the future. I'm concerned that if I die somebody might come along and trick her out of our insurance money and other assets.

ANSWER:

There's nothing wrong with leaving assets in a trust for your spouse. In many instances, if the person doesn't really want to be bothered with the management of the money, it's a good financial planning tool.

However, I must caution you about something. If you're committing these assets (including the income) to be used only for your widow, in my opinion, that is unscriptural. If your wife remarries, she is bound to her new husband and they are to be *one*. And whatever assets she has available should also be available to him.

I understand the argument against that very well: What if she marries a scoundrel? Well, you have to trust her judgment, and she has to be smart enough not to marry a scoundrel, but once married they are to be one person, with no barrier between them. If you leave this money only to her and her future husband has no access to it, even for living expenses, you have created an artificial barrier between them.

The apostle Paul said, *"Wives, be subject to your own husbands, as to the Lord"* (Ephesians 5:22). As a Christian, you don't want to be guilty of interfering in a future relationship. So you need to discuss this with your wife and have a clear understanding. Ultimately, if you do leave it in trust, make the trust flexible enough that her future husband can have access to the funds.

I know that this counsel runs contrary to most of the advice in our generation, but that advice is based primarily on what the world says, not on what God's Word says.

QUESTION:
Should husbands and wives ever keep their assets separate?

ANSWER:
A great thing about God's Word is that it is clear and concise, and it doesn't regard ages, assets, or opinions. According to God's Word, once you're married, you and your new husband are one. Period.

If you both willingly agree to keep the assets separate, that's fine. However, you need to be very sure that neither of you is doing this because of intimidation—either from each other or from other members of the family. I'm concerned that if you keep your assets separate your marriage will suffer. Spend some time praying about this, seeking God's plan for your life, and seeking some good counsel.

God has given the leadership of the home to the husband, and you as his wife are to honor him, as he is to love you unreservedly. I trust that after you pray about this and seek God's wisdom you'll be in agreement about the distribution of these assets.

QUESTION:

How can we convey to my parents that constantly giving money to us is not the right thing to do?

My parents are wealthy, but we really don't want their money and we don't need it. In fact, in some ways I think it is a hindrance to our being good managers of our own resources, because every time we set up a budget to try to discipline ourselves they just dump money on us. I love my parents and don't want to hurt their feelings.

ANSWER:

The solution is not going to be easy, but the best thing to do is to be totally honest with them. Let them know that you're trying to manage your money and live on what you make. Ask them to put the money into a trust, where you don't have access to it until you're ready to manage it. Be very careful with them. Let them know that you care about them and that you appreciate what they're trying to do but that you have a responsibility to be good managers of your own money.

"It is required of stewards that one be found trustworthy . . . The one who examines me is the Lord" (1 Corinthians 4:2, 4).

2

BUDGETING

We all have a budget in one fashion or another. For some couples, it means they spend until all the money for that month is gone, but they determine not to overspend. That plan seems to work until the car breaks down or they lose a job for a while. Then they rationalize the use of debt as a necessity they couldn't avoid.

Some couples spend all they make and rely on credit cards to fund the monthly deficits. They realize they have a problem but rationalize that they just don't make enough money to get by.

A smaller segment of the population makes enough money to be sloppy and get away with it. They may overspend, buying expensive indulgences, but they can cut back and pay their way out without much pain. However, they also are the ones who wonder how they can earn so much but never seem to have any money.

The goal for those who want to be good stewards is to live by a plan that balances their earnings with their spending—in other words, a *budget*.

A budget is a simple plan that divides the available income (after taxes and tithes) into the common categories of spending (Housing, Auto, Food, and the like—see the Percentage Guide for Family Income on page 119, which lists all the budget categories). Spending has to include what doesn't come due every month (clothing, vacations, car repairs, and so on).

QUESTION:

How can we get started on a budget and get ourselves out of debt?

My husband and I have been struggling to get on a budget and have tried several times, but they never seem to work for us.

ANSWER:

There is really no easy answer except to do it. The reason most people's budgets don't work is because they continue to spend more money than they make on a month-by-month basis. If this is your problem, you'll need to solve that first. No budget will work until you commit to living on no more than you make.

Go through each budget category shown in our Percentage Guide table (see page 119) and compare it to your own spending. For instance, if the Housing category (which includes payments, taxes, utilities, maintenance) for your income allocates 35 percent of your income and your budget is consuming, let's say, 60 percent on Housing, your budget won't work. The logical solution to that problem is to sell your house, move into a less expensive one, and get your budget percentage back in line. There's really no other way it will work.

A second problem that many people run into is that they set up their budget properly as recommended, and then they find out the first month that it doesn't work because they allocated $25 to car repairs, but they had a $150 car bill. The only way that most budgets will work is over the long term. Remember that you didn't get into debt in one month, and you're not going to get out of debt in one month.

But if you'll stick to the budget, it will work. At first, you might have to get that $150 for car repair by robbing every other category. However, if you'll stick to the plan and start paying those categories back, within about one year you'll find that you have the surpluses to meet emergencies in the various categories.

When you start your budget, you have to tailor it to you and your husband; our guidelines are only recommendations. The bottom line with any budget is that when you add all of your percentages, the total cannot exceed 100 percent.

You must also be realistic. Many people try to make their budget work by allocating zero for things like Entertainment/Recreation, Clothing, Miscellaneous, or some other category. This won't work. Not one couple has ever shown up for counseling naked; therefore, I knew they had to have money in their budget for clothing. And yet many budgets allocate nothing for clothing. It may mean that you have to modify your buying habits for clothes, but you do have to have something in every budget category.

Many people say, "We never take a vacation." But most people do, and if you don't allocate money for it, your budget simply won't work. So, be realistic.

QUESTION:
Our budget is working and we have some money saved, so where's the best place to put the savings and how do we allocate it?

Answer:

Since you need to keep it readily available, I recommend that you set up a money market account at your local bank or a brokerage firm. Money market accounts will pay the most interest, and the money is available as needed. For instance, if you have your money in a checking account, you're probably making 1 to 2 percent on it; if you have it in a savings account, you may be making 3 to 4 percent; but if you put it in a money market account, you could be making 5 to 6 percent. Most money market accounts will allow you to write checks on the money in your account.

As far as allocating the savings, remember that the money is there for a purpose, and your Savings Account Allocation form in the back (see page 120) reflects that purpose. Let's assume, arbitrarily, that you have $1,000 in a money market account, but $100 is for clothing, $100 for travel, $100 is for miscellaneous, and so on. In other words, the money is allocated, and when you look at the Savings Account form it should reflect that you have $100 available to spend on clothing, miscellaneous, and so forth. Therefore, this money is budgeted and allocated like any other category. The money can stay in one account, but it has to be allocated by use.

Question:

How do we decide if something is a need, want, or desire?

We don't have a debt problem. We have the money to buy pretty much whatever we want, so money is not a problem. But I find our spending is continuing to increase along with our income, and that concerns me.

Answer:

You have a problem that lots of people would like to have, or at least they think they would. And you're right: It is difficult to deal with. I think of what the prophet Agur said in Proverbs: *"Two things I asked of You, do not refuse me before I die: Keep deception and lies far from me, give me neither poverty nor riches; feed me with the food that is my portion, that I not be full and deny You and say, 'Who is the LORD?' or that I not be in want and steal, and profane the name of my God"* (Proverbs 30:7–9).

For better or worse, you fit in the category of having riches. It's a great position to be in if you have a heart for giving, but a bad position to be in if you have a heart for spending. It's very difficult to discern what is a need, want, or desire. Let me explain.

When you're about to buy something and the price is not the determining factor, you need to ask yourself, "Is not having this causing a lack in my life?"

Let me give you an example: If you were a carpenter you would need a hammer. Hammers and nails are not very expensive, and for a carpenter they're necessary for making a living. But if you're an earthmover, you might need a bulldozer. A bulldozer often costs hundreds of thousands of dollars. The amount it costs isn't the real issue; it's what you're going to do with it.

So, before you buy, ask yourself, "Will this thing I'm considering have utility in my life?" I find that most people buy things that have little or no utility in their lives and they end up in storage or parked in their backyards, gathering rotten leaves. That includes motor homes, boats, airplanes, and all kinds of toys that we buy.

Pray about this and decide if your life is suffering as a result of not having whatever you're about to buy.

Remember, God has ordained some of your surplus to help others. *"He who is gracious to a poor man lends to the LORD, and He will repay him for his good deed"* (Proverbs 19:17).

QUESTION:
How can we stay on a budget when our income has been reduced by almost half?

My husband lost his job. He's now employed, but he's only making half of what he was in his previous job. We realize we need to make some changes, but we're not sure where to start. It seems so overwhelming.

ANSWER:
There's no easy way to do this except to be realistic. One of the difficulties I find with many people whose income has been reduced—and that's always a possibility in our volatile economy—is that they aren't willing to face the facts. The fact is, they don't make as much money as they used to make; therefore, the second fact is, they can't spend as much money as they used to spend.

You have to take a realistic approach to where you are financially. Look at every category—Housing, Automobile, Food, Entertainment/Recreation, and the others—and bring those percentages down until you can live within the available income (and remember the total can be no more than 100 percent). It may mean selling your home or scaling down the cars. It also may mean not taking a vacation for a period of time or taking a semester off from graduate school, but that's what reality is all about.

And remember, whatever you're making, there are probably millions of other couples out there making even less and living on it.

QUESTION:

Why do we end up at the end of the month without enough money when we have a budget?

We've been working on our budget now for several months and, on paper, when we plot our income and spending, it looks okay, but at the end of the month we don't have enough money to meet all our needs. I don't understand what our problem is.

ANSWER:

In practical truth, you have made out what I call the idealistic budget. You've programmed everything based on income, but you're not controlling your spending. You have to let the budget control what you're spending.

For instance, let's say you are using the envelope method of budgeting. You have an Entertainment/Recreation monthly budget of $200, and you get paid twice per month. That means that in each pay period you would put $100 into your Entertainment/ Recreation envelope. When you go out for entertainment, you take your envelope with you and you pay for whatever you do (eating out, movies) out of the envelope and put the change back in. This way you know exactly what you have left. But when you look in the envelope and it's empty, then you must stop spending in that category until you get paid again.

That principle works with every category of budgeting. It's not complicated; it is what's called self-discipline.

QUESTION:

Can you give me some scriptural reasons why we should budget?

My husband listens to you, and he says that we need a budget, but I don't see the purpose. I manage our money very well, I don't spend more than we make, and I think a budget is far too restrictive.

ANSWER:

"The mind of a man plans his way, but the LORD directs his steps" (Proverbs 16:9). God expects us to be participants in planning our budget, not observers. The purpose of budgeting is to free your mind of financial worries; it is not supposed to be a self-inflicted punishment.

I'm not trying to make your life miserable. All I can do is offer some good counsel to Christians, the majority of whom don't manage money very well. You should be free from worrying about whether your annual insurance is paid on time, whether you put money aside for the taxes on your house, and whether you have enough money to educate your children when it's time for college.

If those areas are not problems for you, then you're among the fortunate few in America. Even when you live within your income, you can still be spending too much money.

I never go into debt—never have, never will. But from time to time I find myself spending a lot more money than I need to spend and more than I probably should spend. So my budget is for the purpose of monitoring my self-discipline.

Scriptural guidelines for budgeting can be found throughout God's Word. For instance, *"Know well the condition of your flocks, and pay attention to your herds; for riches are not forever"* (Proverbs

27:23). If you don't happen to have any flocks and herds, probably God is saying to know well the condition of your clothing allowance, housing budget, and your food budget.

Another positive aspect is that a budget can help you and your husband develop better communication. If he wants to live on a budget, he obviously sees a need to do so. He wants to be a better steward of the money God has provided the two of you. And you, as his helpmate, should be willing to sit down with him, discuss this, and then come to some reasonable compromise.

Your budget probably won't need to control your spending to the exact dollar every month, nor should it, but there should be some reasonable way for you to work this out together. All a budget can do is show how much money you're making and help you decide where you're going to spend it. That's neither complicated nor confining—except within the limits of your income and God's will.

I believe that everybody needs a budget. Ten percent of our population make enough money to be sloppy and get away with it; 10 percent are so cheap they'll probably never overspend; but the other 80 percent will get themselves into deep trouble. Remember, financial problems are the number one cause of family conflicts in America today.

QUESTION:

How do I budget my husband's income when it is so irregular, and how much of his travel expenses should be included in our family budget?

My husband is a trucker, he's rarely home, and his income is irregular (when he's working certain times of the year his income is high; other times it's very low).

ANSWER:

First, you need to keep two entirely separate budgets. If your husband is a self-employed contractor (truck driver), you need to set aside the taxes (in a separate account) and pay them on a quarterly basis. You also need a budget just for the business. The money that's left after all the business expenses have been paid becomes income for the two of you—or profit—so, you also need a second budget for your marriage.

Since the income is variable, I would recommend that you do the following. Figure how much he makes annually, divide that by twelve, and that becomes your monthly income. Set up a savings account or a money market account and deposit all the family funds into that account. From that account, you'll pay the personal taxes that are due; then the amount left over becomes your monthly budget.

Let's assume that your estimated income is $24,000 per year, or $2,000 per month. All money earned (after business expenses) goes into the savings account; then once a month you withdraw $2,000 to pay your household expenses. That's the only way you'll be able to make this budget work.

You have to take your variable income and make it appear to be a more regular income. That means that during the high-income months you store the money so that during the low-income months you can draw from that pool. The vast majority of the people who have a variable income—commission or otherwise—

end up spending all the money during the higher-income months, because they treat it like a windfall profit. Then during the bad times they don't have any reserves and go into debt. You don't want that to happen to you.

QUESTION:
How do I convince my husband that we should start living on a budget?

I've been listening to your program for several years now, and I am convicted to get on a budget, but I don't think our budget is going to work. We always spend more than we make, and it seems like every time we get a raise the money is consumed before we even get it. My husband is not interested in working on a budget with me. He says it's too depressing. Any ideas?

ANSWER:
The reason it's depressing to your husband is because he's not facing reality. The time to start a budget is now! Don't wait until you get out of debt, because without a budget you probably aren't going to get out of debt. I'd suggest asking your husband (as sweetly as you can), "I really would like to get on a budget, but I can't do it without your help. Will you work with me?"

If he says yes, then all you need to get started are the additional resources at the end of this chapter. We also have many volunteer counselors through Crown Ministries—perhaps we have one in your area.

If he says no, you have to be willing to be blunt and turn the finances over to him. Be honest and tell him the truth—that you can't handle the pressure and it is really his responsibility. Explain that you're more than willing to help but that you can't do it alone. That's the only way you're going to be able to deal with this problem. Remember, in a marriage, it takes both of you working on the problem or else it won't be solved. To attempt to handle this alone will result in a lot of frustration.

"Two are better than one because they have a good return for their labor. For if either of them falls, the one will lift up his companion. But woe to the one who falls when there is not another to lift him up" (Ecclesiastes 4:9–10).

QUESTION:
How can we get out of debt and stay out?

In our marriage we live paycheck to paycheck. We never have any accumulated surplus, and we live on credit cards. If we get a large bonus or something, we get ourselves nearly out of debt, but then we just get right back in again. Any suggestions?

ANSWER:
There is no alternative but to get on a good financial plan—for a family, it's called a budget. First, you need to take a realistic look at what you're spending versus what you're making and then decide how to make the two compatible. If you can't increase your income, and most people can't, then you must decrease your spending. And that requires some difficult choices.

Sometimes it means selling a home. Sometimes it means getting by with a single car—not very convenient today. Sometimes it means not taking vacations for a period of time or else taking short trips. Other times it means shopping in thrift shops for your clothes and shopping in discount stores for gifts. That's not a lot of fun, and it's humbling for most people, but sometimes that's what it takes to make a budget work. If you're willing to sacrifice, a budget will work, regardless of your income.

I've counseled with people who made $200,000 a year, others who made $100,000, some who made $50,000, and others who made only $20,000. Most of them said the same thing initially: They didn't make enough money. If the income of the couple with $20,000 had suddenly been raised to $100,000, they would have thought they were wealthy, but if they didn't change their habits, within a couple of years they would be spending it all. It's a matter of facing the problems realistically and deciding that you really want to solve them.

QUESTION:
What's the difference between what you call your savings plan and an emergency plan?

ANSWER:
Within the budget there are several categories of savings. For instance, the Automobile category has a savings category for car repairs, tire replacement—those types of things. Within the Clothing category there is savings for seasonal clothing. When those monies are saved, they're allocated to a specific category.

However, in addition, I recommend that a budget include an emergency savings account, which is a surplus of money that's available for unforeseen contingencies. For instance, if you lost your job, you would have that money to fall back on. I recommend saving about six months' income, if possible, but not less than three months'.

In addition, you should have a category of savings that could be called Long-Term Savings for the Future, such as money put aside for your children's college education or perhaps retirement.

So, in essence, a well-managed budget would have three categories of savings: one for individual categories of spending within your budget—Housing, Clothing, Food, Automobile, and so forth. The second would be emergency savings for unplanned contingencies. And the third would be for long-term planned events. *"Divide your portion to seven, or even to eight, for you do not know what misfortune may occur on the earth"* (Ecclesiastes 11:2).

QUESTION:

What can we do if we don't have enough money to meet our month-to-month bills and also pay our creditors?

We've started your budget, but our difficulty is that we've cut back as much as we can, and we still don't have enough money to go around. If we don't pay the creditors, obviously we're going to get into financial trouble. In fact, we have some credit card companies threatening to sue us right now. What are our alternatives?

ANSWER:

First, you need to be sure that your budget is realistic. If you think you've trimmed it as far as it can be trimmed and you can't get it down any further, get some help. It probably can be reduced more. Also, perhaps you can contact your creditors and work out an alternative payment plan that doesn't require as much money per month. Some of them will work with you, but many of them, I suspect, will not. Therefore, you'll need some outside help.

I recommend using one of the credit counseling companies—like Consumer Credit Counseling Service—and have them help you work out a plan with your creditors. They almost always can help you not only reduce the payments but also reduce the interest as well. (See the additional resources at the end of this chapter.) We work with a group in Atlanta that handles the entire nation via telephone for us, and it works very well.

But stick to your plan, pay what you can, and don't give up. You're doing the right thing, and God is still in control.

"Commit your works to the LORD, and your plans will be established. The LORD has made everything for its own purpose" (Proverbs 16:3–4).

QUESTION:
Should our budget be a source of strife?

My husband and I began a budget several months ago, but it seems like whatever we do, we do to the extreme. My husband is so committed to this budget that he allows me no flexibility whatsoever. We've eliminated all Entertainment/Recreation, all Clothing, and even sold my car. Now he's seriously considering selling our home and moving into a small apartment, even though I believe we'll be okay where we are. He says that we're not saving enough for the future.

ANSWER:
The best counsel that I can give has been given by God in Genesis 2:24, where God said He created a husband and a wife to be one

person. That means that any budget worked out in a marriage has to work for both people, not just one. A common mistake in budgeting is to try to overcorrect, based on the dominant person's personality. These kinds of budgets work well on paper, but they don't work very well in real life. I suggest that your husband needs to reach a better balance.

I saw this principle demonstrated some time ago when I was counseling a financial analyst and his wife. He could analyze a company's financial report, but he didn't know how to balance his own checkbook. After our second counseling session, I gave them a task of developing a budget to control their Miscellaneous spending (that's the category that eats up your money and you can never remember where it went).

In their case, they were overspending nearly $300 a month on a variety of miscellaneous things, such as boats and trips. When they returned, about two months later, I asked the husband, "How do you like your plan so far?"

His response was, "This is great. We now have our spending under control. We've stopped going any further into debt. In fact, we're paying off some debt and we have a little savings."

Then I asked his wife, "How do you like your plan so far?"

She replied, "This is absolutely the worst thing that has ever happened in my life."

"Why is that?" I asked.

"I thought you told me this would be a plan that would work for both of us."

I responded, "Absolutely."

"Well," she said, "let me tell you something. He's decided that my hair appointment is miscellaneous, our clothes are miscellaneous, my car is miscellaneous, our house is miscellaneous." She went on to name the things that he had trimmed out of their budget. "But," she said, "his boat is not miscellaneous. And when the motor broke and we had to spend $200 on it, he said it was a necessity."

Obviously, that husband had made out a budget that worked very well for one person. Unfortunately, there was another person in the marriage, and therefore the budget had to work for both of them. I shared a scriptural reference that I thought would help their situation perfectly: *"The way of a fool is right in his own eyes, but a wise man is he who listens to counsel"* (Proverbs 12:15). The primary counselor of any husband is his wife. The primary counselor of any wife is her husband.

I recommend that you work through a third party—a counselor—and get the situation under control. No budget should create the strife you two are having.

ADDITIONAL RESOURCES

The Savings Account Allocation form is one example of the many types of useful resources available to help you develop a Crown Financial Ministries budget. See page 120.

Budgeting helps available from Crown Financial Ministries and your local Christian bookstore include the following:

- *Money Matters Deluxe* software with Larry Burkett's time-proven guidelines for successful budgeting, biblical counsel on related financial topics, expense tracking by budget category, and *SnapShot Gold* software.

- Crown has many other helpful resources for you. Check our Web site, www.crown.org, or call toll-free (800) 722-1976 for more information.
- Budget counseling referral service is a lay ministry of volunteer budget counselors, the local church, and Crown Financial Ministries. There is no fee for this service (you have the option of purchasing workbooks that will enhance your study of godly stewardship, but you are under no obligation to purchase any item). Counselors have completed Crown's budget counselor's study course, and they help God's people set up budgets and learn how to honor the Lord with their finances. To receive an application for a referral counselor by e-mail, just send a blank e-mail to counselor@crown.org (we do not read messages sent to this address). You will receive an auto-response with further directions. You may call (800) 722-1976 or write to Crown Financial Ministries, 601 Broad St. SE, Gainesville, GA 30501-3790.

If you need the assistance of a mediator with creditors, often organizations such as Consumer Credit Counseling Service can help. You may contact Consumer Credit Counseling Service at (800) 251-CCCS or www.cccsatl.org.

3

HOUSING AND AUTOMOBILES

ousing is the largest single expense category for most couples. It also represents the biggest problem area for most couples. Expectations in the current generation demand a home that most people only dreamed about a generation ago. Available long-term loans have made expensive housing the norm, rather than the exception.

However, what people can buy and what they can afford are generally at odds today. Lenders often look at two incomes when qualifying home buyers, which is unfortunate because children frequently come along after the home is purchased, and one of those two incomes is interrupted.

In reality, many buyers consume 60 percent or more of their income on their homes. There is virtually no way they can balance their budgets with such a large percentage committed to one category. The question is often asked, "What do we do now?"

The purchase of an automobile is the second largest expense that most couples will incur in their lifetimes. In reality, if you take the cumulative total of automobiles purchased during the life span of most people, it may well be the largest single expense that most of them incur. And that's especially true when you factor in the associated costs of maintenance, gasoline, insurance, and other expenses. It's important for most couples to understand the consequences of making good financial decisions about automobiles.

I believe I can say without fear of contradiction that the vast majority of Americans are living well beyond their automobile budgets. They buy new cars when they really can afford only used cars; they finance their cars without any expectations of ever owning a car debt free; and most of them are more concerned with the monthly payments than they are with the retail cost of their cars.

Also, in my opinion, car leases are the worst deals available for nonbusiness car buyers.

HOUSING

QUESTION:
Is it better to buy or to rent?

We have been married six years, we're still renting, and I'm concerned that we're just throwing our money away. My husband says that he can make more money by investing the funds that we would otherwise put into a home. However, totally outside of the area of investing, I would like to have a home for our family.

ANSWER:
We're really dealing with a couple of issues here. In the area of buying versus renting a home, the budget is really the key. The question you have to ask is, "Can we afford to buy, considering

what our net cost would be?" In other words, when you rent you know what your net outlay is: the amount of money you pay per month, since you don't get to write any of it off.

When you buy, there are some expenses that you can deduct from your income tax (if you itemize). This includes the interest you pay on the loan and the real estate taxes. So you're really concerned about the *net* amount you're paying to buy a home.

Basically, if you can afford to buy for what it costs to rent per month, in my opinion, you're better off buying, because you can't accumulate equity in rent. All things being equal, therefore, it is better for most families to buy rather than to rent. However, if your rent is substantially cheaper than what it would cost to make house payments, and your budget is limited to what you are now paying in rent, obviously it would be better for you to rent.

The other issue is whether it's better to invest, as opposed to buying a home. It has been my observation that, for the majority of people who decide to invest the difference, most don't do very well. A few people are committed investors who stick to the plan, but the majority of people who have money available in an investment plan, other than a qualified retirement plan like a 401(k) or an IRA, often end up spending the money. Again, remember the bottom line: It's better to buy, but only if it fits your budget.

QUESTION:
Should we buy a home in the town where my husband will be attending college for two years?

We decided that he needs to go back to grad school to improve his education, so we sold our home. If we shouldn't buy a home in the town where the college is located, what should we do with the money from the sale of our house until he gets out of grad school?

ANSWER:
Generally speaking, three years in one location is the minimal amount of time for buying a home. The reason for that is when you move into a new area you need time to decide where you want to buy. Then you have to qualify and purchase a home. Then, when you're ready to leave, it takes time to sell the home. There's always the chance that it might not be the best time in the economy, so you might not be able to sell it immediately; then you're stuck with a house in a location where you don't want to live. So, if you're not going to be there more than three years, I would say don't buy a house.

However, if you can find a really good buy in the college town—less than what you'd pay in rent—then it might be worth the risk, particularly if it is a property that you know is easily sellable to another student.

If you don't buy a house, though, don't take big risks with this money. The money is there for you to buy another home and, therefore, should be secured. I personally would put my money in a money market account with one of the large brokerage firms, maximize the interest I could earn on it, and not take risks with it.

QUESTION:
Is it better to put more of our money down on the home we're going to buy or just a little bit down?

ANSWER:
If you can pay 100 percent on your home, I believe it's better to

do that. You don't make money by borrowing somebody else's money. If you don't believe that, just look around at the biggest buildings in your city. They're usually banks.

However, in reality, when you're buying a home, if you can't put 100 percent down and own the house debt free, you're probably better off not using all your cash assets. In other words, put down enough to afford the payments.

One issue that you need to consider is Private Mortgage Insurance (PMI). If you have 20 percent equity in your home you can avoid the PMI, which typically adds 1 percent to your mortgage cost per year. So if you're financing a $100,000 home, you'll pay about $1,000 per year in PMI, but with 20 percent equity or greater you can avoid paying it.

Otherwise, just consider that you're buying the home in lieu of rent—in other words, you're buying the home as a substitute to renting, in which case it's better to put a small amount of money down. The other question I would ask is, Do you plan to stay in this home long term? If you do want to own the home, then it would be better to put more money down. In fact, try to accelerate the payments on your home on a monthly basis.

QUESTION:
How much can we afford to pay on our home mortgage?

Our lender has qualified us at about 40 percent of our gross income. When I calculate the payments, it seems awfully high for us to afford on a $40,000 salary.

ANSWER:
In my opinion, 40 percent is the maximum that should ever be qualified, but it's 40 percent of your Net Spendable Income (that's income

minus taxes and tithe). And remember that 40 percent, in our budget system, must include your mortgage payments, taxes, utilities, maintenance, telephone bills—every expense associated with your home.

Also bear in mind that the number one financial problem facing most young couples is that they spend too much on their housing. In reality, based on your income, your housing allowance at $40,000 in income should be around 35 percent of your Net Spendable Income (after taxes and tithes). Many young couples are spending 60 to 65 percent of their total income on their homes, and that's why their budgets won't balance.

In the area of housing, it's better to do with less—initially. Buy a smaller home until you can handle a larger home more comfortably—that is, when income increases. Actually, if you buy a home that is within your budget and you can control your other expenses, you should be able to pay off the mortgage in about seven years. Obviously, for the majority of young couples today, that is virtually impossible. They can't pay their homes off in 100 years, because they have overcommitted.

Question:
Should we use a home equity loan to consolidate our debt?

We've gotten ourselves into severe debt problems. We owe about $17,000 in credit cards; we still owe about $10,000 in school loans; and now we owe doctor bills that probably amount to more than $12,000. We don't have that much equity in our home, but we do have about $30,000. Should we borrow the money out of our home to consolidate as many of these debts as possible so that we can make our payments on a timely basis?

Answer:

There's at least one positive factor when you use your home to consolidate a loan: The interest is deductible. In reality, debt is debt. But having said that, there are some prerequisites that you must meet before I would recommend that you use your home equity to consolidate debts. You need to make sure that you're treating the problem and not the symptom. The symptom is the debt that you owe: credit cards, school loans, and doctor bills. The problem is, you're living beyond your means.

So I would first recommend that you get on a budget and live on it for at least six months, making the current payment schedule that you now have. If you can't make the current payment schedule because you're too far in debt, in all probability a consolidation loan will not solve the problem; it will merely treat the symptom. You need to pray about this together and agree together on the sacrifices necessary to pay down this debt.

One of the things I recommend, particularly when dealing with credit cards, is that you make an agreement like the one on the following page and tape it on your refrigerator.

Lord, from this day forward we will pay off any new credit card purchases each month, without interest. The first month we fail to meet this promise we will destroy all our credit cards.

Husband   _____

Wife   _____

Date   _____

Basically, you're promising that the next time you use your credit cards and don't pay off the current charges that month, you'll destroy them. Without this commitment, all the consolidation loans will do is ease the pressure you're under right now. And within a year, or two at the most, you'll be right back in the same trouble you're in now, only you'll owe a consolidation loan in addition to the other debts.

Let me assure you that I've seen many couples who consolidated their debts, using their home equity or something else, and they went right back into the same difficulty—only worse. Often, the next time it ended up in something more severe—like bankruptcy or divorce.

From this day forward, you must make a commitment to incur no more debt, no matter what the circumstances. I believe that you also need to make yourselves accountable to somebody else. I would suggest you go to your pastor and see if he can suggest a good budget counselor in your church who will work with you. If you're willing to do this, perhaps the consolidation loan is a reasonable thing to do.

Question:
We want to build a home debt free, but is it a good thing to do?

I've been listening to your radio program for many years now. We've been married for two years, and I have told my wife that I am committed to the Larry Burkett principle of being totally debt free, including our home. We're not going to build a home until we can pay cash for it. My wife doesn't agree with this and wants your opinion.

ANSWER:

The answer to this question is best answered by you and your wife. It is possible to build a home debt free, but certain things are required: great communication and cooperation between husband and wife. Another is being willing to sacrifice virtually everything else for five to seven years. And remember that both of you must be committed to this project totally; you must pray about it together and have no reservations, because it's going to be a very difficult thing to do. You'll need to save enough money to buy the land for cash, and you'll have to be willing to do much of the work on the house yourself in order to keep the expenses down.

Obviously you have to have surplus money to be able to do this. I would say it is unrealistic for a couple with children to accomplish this. So if you have no children, and if you're willing to take no vacations, do away with your Entertainment/Recreation budget, and make a commitment to buy no new cars during this process, you might be able to do it. For the majority of couples, I would say this is not the way to go. It's not for everybody.

I jokingly say something that's not really a joke: Unless you have been married for ten years you probably shouldn't even try to build a home, much less try to build a home debt free. Perhaps the compromise that you could make is to finance your first home, accumulate enough cash that you can buy the land for cash, and then try to use the equity plus whatever surplus you have above that to build your next home debt free.

Even then, without both of you being absolutely committed to this, it will not work. I have known several young couples who set out to build a home debt free. The majority of them did not succeed. About 1 in 20 actually stuck it out. And, unfortunately, in some cases their marriages did not make it either. So, as I said, it's not for everybody.

Two staff members of Crown Financial Ministries have built debt-free homes. They discovered it could be done because they and their spouses were willing to be totally committed to the concept. Though it was difficult, they had the resolve to put in a lot of sweat equity, and they sacrificed in the short term in order to enjoy the future benefits of debt-free homes.

QUESTION:
Should we buy our home using a conventional or a government loan?

We're looking at buying our first home and are checking into mortgage rates. It seems to us that buying a home through the FHA or VA is a less expensive way. Can you tell me if there are any downsides to this?

ANSWER:
In most instances government loans will be cheaper, at least initially. They require less down payment: typically about 5 percent (or zero) down, depending on the type of loan you get. But, in reality, many conventional loans today are very competitive and offer the same interest rates—and many times the same money down. In fact, there are conventional loans available that will lend you more than 100 percent of the total loan amount. I don't recommend these loans.

Basically though, the bottom line is that it doesn't matter what kind of loan you get, if you know that you can work it into your budget and that you can afford the payments on the home.

Question:

What is the best way to pay off our mortgage early?

We would like to retire our thirty-year mortgage early.

Answer:

The best method to prepay your mortgage is to make additional prepayments monthly. For instance, you make your regular payment; then you write a second check, made payable to "principal only." And, you do need to verify, at least annually, that all of the payments have been credited properly. Otherwise your bank may take your prepayment and allocate it as part of the next regular monthly payment, in which case interest would be taken out of it, and you don't want that.

The chart below shows a $100,000 loan, financed at 7 percent for thirty years, and shows how paying an extra $50 per month can retire that note early and how much interest it will save you.

	Original Mortgage	**With Extra $50 Payment**
Interest Paid	$139,511.00	$107,855.81
Term	30 years	24 years 3 months
Total Payments	360	291
Interest Saved		$31,655.19
Total Time Saved		5 years 9 months
Payments Eliminated		69

Increase the extra payment amount to $100 and you'll save $50,508.27 in interest and eliminate a total of 114 payments (that's 9- 1/2 years). The benefit of paying any extra amount has a powerful leveraging effect on savings returned to you.

Mortgage loans are simple-interest loans, meaning that the interest is calculated on the unpaid balance at the beginning of the month; therefore, you do have prepayment privileges. And the more principal you pay down, the less interest you pay in the next payment as well. The advantage of prepaying, using this method, is that there are no up-front fees.

QUESTION:
Are condominiums a good value?

We're a newly married young couple looking for a place to live, and housing in our area is very expensive. We looked at condos and found that they are much less expensive—by about one-third—but we're not sure about the resale value.

Answer:
Usually, the purchase of any property, including a condominium, depends on the area of the country and what's going on in your economy. There are areas, such as South Florida and some of the recreational areas, where condos sell just as readily as homes; but, in other areas condos do not sell as readily as homes, even at lower costs.

Also remember that there are some additional costs associated with condos, such as the association fees you must pay every month. Because you're in a complex that is physically linked to other units, you must pay common fees for the upkeep of the grounds, the roofs, and the buildings. Sometimes these fees are substantial, so you need to verify what they are before you buy.

Another factor to remember is that since the sale of condos is somewhat more difficult, you don't want to buy one if you're going to have to move often (for instance, if you're a military person or perhaps a pastor who moves a lot).

If you only plan to rent a condo, typically they do cost less than a stand-alone home. However, if you're buying a condominium in an area where you plan to live for a reasonable period of time and you can get a good deal, in my opinion, condos can be an excellent bargain for many people.

What I believe makes a condo particularly attractive is that you don't have much personal maintenance and upkeep, because much of that is done by the homeowners' association. Anytime you don't have yard work or maintenance, I'm for that!

AUTOMOBILES

QUESTION:

Is it a good idea to lease an automobile?

We're getting ready to buy a new automobile. My husband is a salesman and needs a good car in order to do his day-to-day routine. Unfortunately, we don't have enough money saved to buy an automobile for cash; neither do we have enough money to make a down payment on a vehicle. Do you think that a lease is a good alternative for couples like us?

ANSWER:

In my opinion, because of the depreciation on the automobile as soon as you drive it off the lot, buying a brand-new car, by whatever means, is not a good deal for the majority of people. Typically, a new automobile will depreciate between 15 and 25 percent of its initial value, depending on the type of car and the retail price, just as a result of titling the vehicle. That's a lot of depreciation for most people when you figure that a $30,000 automobile may lose as much as $7,000 to $8,000 of its value just as a result of your purchase. That doesn't seem like a good deal to me.

Further, the difficulty with buying new automobiles is simply compounded in a lease. This is because the dealer and the manufacturer are going to make a profit on each automobile, whether you buy it outright for cash, buy it with a loan, or lease it. The difficulty I see with leasing an automobile is that you usually are paying maximum retail price for the vehicle and financing it at high market rates. And, in the end, you *still don't own it.*

Unfortunately, most people are not even concerned with what a vehicle costs them. All they're concerned about is the monthly payments; and the same is true if they lease. When an automobile is leased, the contract carries with it penalties for excessive mileage—mileage in excess of what was agreed to in the contract, which is usually around 15,000 miles per year. Many Americans today will put more than 15,000 miles a year on a vehicle, so when they return the car, after the lease period, they owe mileage penalties. They also may owe wear penalties—that's a penalty to cover the excessive amount of wear and tear on the automobile (in the leaseholder's opinion).

Another thing to remember is that signing a lease is just as binding as signing a contract to buy a car. If you want to get out of the lease early, you'll owe early payoff penalties on the vehicle, plus whatever wear and tear is assessed.

One caution I offer to anyone who is already driving a leased vehicle: Don't allow any other person, friend or otherwise, to assume your lease. Your name is still on that contract, and if that person doesn't pay, you're going to pay. If the car has been abused, you'll be stuck with the bill for the wear and tear as well.

Bottom line, I don't believe that leased automobiles are an especially good deal. In fact, for most individuals outside of the business environment, leases are a very bad deal. Normally, I don't recommend leasing a car.

God's Word says, *"Which one of you, when he wants to build a tower, does not first sit down and calculate the cost, to see if he has enough to complete it?"* (Luke 14:28). Most people don't consider the total cost.

QUESTION:

Is it better to keep an old car and repair it or trade for a new one?

My husband and I drive two old cars, one with 150,000 miles and the other with over 180,000 miles. At what point should we decide that it's no longer profitable to keep these old cars and trade them in for new ones? I've heard you say many times that the cheapest vehicle to drive is the one you're driving, but is that always true? Don't cars eventually wear out?

ANSWER:

Yes, you're absolutely right. There is a point at which it's a losing proposition to try to maintain an old automobile. That's particularly true with a car that has in excess of 200,000 miles, because often at that stage metal fatigue sets in and the car begins to disintegrate.

In general, though, the cheapest car to drive *is* the one you are driving. Of course, that will depend on the specific car you own (some cars are just better than others), how much mileage it has, and your use of the automobile. If you just drive your vehicle around town, a breakdown might not be a major catastrophe. However, if you drive it long distances and use it to make a living, that's something else.

Let me mention another point: If you're trading in an old vehicle, generally you're better off to sell it on your own or give it to a nonprofit organization (and write it off on your income tax) than you are trading it in. Usually, if you trade in an old automobile, the dealer will appear to give you something for it but actually will mark up the price of the vehicle you are buying to compensate for it. After all, the dealer has the same problem trying to sell an old used car as you have.

I caution most young couples not to buy new cars. Buy an older car, perhaps one to two years old with a reasonable amount of mileage on it. A two-year-old car with reasonable mileage, in my opinion, would be about 20,000 miles; a one-year-old car, about 10,000 to 12,000 miles. There are very good buys in what are called program cars (some call them demos). These are nearly new cars that have been driven by employees of the dealership. They usually put between 8,000 and 12,000 miles on the vehicles and then resell them. Often you'll get a significant discount on these vehicles (see additional resources at the end of this chapter).

QUESTION:
What do we do with a car that has payments that are too high for us to afford?

About a year ago, we bought a brand-new automobile because our old one was pretty much worn out. We now realize that the payments, almost $190 a month, are far too high for us to afford. However, when we checked the value of the car, we found that we still owe more than the car is worth. What options do we have? Do we have the option to just give the car back and buy another used car?

ANSWER:

No, you can't just give the car back. You have a contract. Your purchase contract may not be with a dealer; it may be with a third-party financier, and the financier doesn't want your car back. If he does get it back, he's going to sell it at a discount and sue you for the difference.

In most instances, you're far better off trying to sell the automobile yourself, with the lender's permission, and surrendering the sales price to the lender. Then you'll have to sign a note for the deficiency (the difference between what you sold the car for and what you still owe on it). But normally, you're going to lose less if you sell the car yourself.

Also remember that when you dispose of a car prematurely, even with the lender's permission, it will go on your credit record for up to seven years, so this is not a thing to take lightly. *"Better is a little with the fear of the LORD, than great treasure and turmoil with it"* (Proverbs 15:16).

QUESTION:

How much should we pay for the new car we are planning to buy?

ANSWER:

If you'll look at the Percentage Guide table on page 119, you'll notice that you should spend no more than 15 percent of your Net

Spendable Income (that's your income after paying taxes and tithes) on your automobile. Note that the percentage includes the expenses to cover the loan payments, insurance, maintenance, fuel—everything that goes into your vehicle, including its eventual replacement.

It's very important to select a car you can afford and not be dazzled by the attraction of new ones. The vast majority of couples earning less than $50,000 a year cannot afford to buy a new car— ever! You should buy a good used vehicle—one you have very carefully selected that will meet your needs.

When I buy an automobile, I first check very thoroughly the model I want. The resources I recommend are *Consumer Reports* magazine, as well as one of the national auto-trade Web sites. Some of these Web sites are listed at the end of this chapter. It's very important that you stay within your budget and select a car you can afford.

"Without consultation, plans are frustrated, but with many counselors they succeed" (Proverbs 15:22).

One of the ways to find a good used car is to ask your friends and family if they have one for sale. Many times they do and just haven't mentioned it. If you can't find one among your friends and family, go to your local newspaper and try to buy from an individual. That way, you can talk to the owner, see the car, and drive it before you make a decision to buy. Plus, in most states, there's no sales tax on private owner sales.

In my opinion, the last place to shop for an automobile is at a dealership, unless you know the dealer personally. It's not that most dealerships are dishonest; they aren't. But remember that they buy these cars at used car auctions and rarely know the total history of the automobile, so you won't know what you're getting.

Question:
What kind of automobile insurance do I need?

My car now has about 100,000 miles on it, and I question whether I need the comprehensive and collision as well as the liability insurance.

Answer:
Obviously, liability insurance is an absolute must, but I believe you're at the breakpoint where collision and comprehensive may not be necessary. However, even a car with 100,000 miles on it needs the collision insurance unless you have enough cash in the bank to fix it in the event of a major accident. Remember, it's not much cheaper to replace a fender on a five-year-old automobile than it is on a one-year-old automobile; the costs are essentially the same.

You might say, "Well, I can drive the older car even though it's banged up." And that's probably true to some degree; however, some of the banging may be so severe that you wouldn't want to drive it around. It might even be dangerous. Liability is a *must;* it's not for your protection, it's for the protection of the people you might hit.

"The prudent sees the evil and hides himself, but the naive go on, and are punished for it" (Proverbs 22:3).

Collision covers the damage on your automobile; comprehensive covers things like glass breakage. In my opinion, comprehensive is probably one of the better buys in automobile insurance. You could do without it, but for what it pays, it's usually worth the cost.

Remember also that if your medical insurance policy excludes automobile injuries, you need to carry some kind of hospitalization health plan on your automobile policy. Before you buy any insurance on your vehicle, shop thoroughly.

When you buy a car, avoid buying your insurance through the dealer or through the lender. Shop for your own insurance. You can use the Web and shop one of the insurance evaluation Web sites listed at the end of this chapter.

ADDITIONAL RESOURCES

Many resources are available that can help you determine the quality, economy, dependability, and affordability of automobiles. Review new and used car values before making a purchase at

- Consumer Reports, www.consumerreports.org
- Kelly Blue Book auto buyers guide, www.kbb.com
- Edmunds, www.edmunds.com
- Cars Direct, www.carsdirect.com

You also can research a car's vehicle identification number (VIN) on-line at

- CarFax, www.carfax.com

Two Internet sites that can help make it easier to research and evaluate automobile insurance are

- Yahoo! Auto Insurance, www.yahoo.com/auto.html
- Excite Auto Insurance, www.excite.com/money/insurance/ auto_insurance

4

DEBT AND CREDIT

The majority of financial questions I'm asked daily deal with the subject of debt and credit. Unfortunately, many of these are tragically similar. Young couples (and older ones too) are caught up in the debt spiral. Often they owe nearly one-third of their total incomes in interest alone.

Thirty years ago credit card debt was fairly new. Twenty years ago it was more common but limited largely to the upper-income, more affluent families. Today it's like a plague spreading through our land with no one—young, old, educated, or illiterate—immune.

Just as the stock market went euphoric (nuts) in the '90s, so did consumer debt. College campuses now allow credit card companies to recruit their students—just as employers do. The result is a new market for high-interest consumer debt, and college students carrying thousands of dollars in credit card debt.

It can be said that capitalism removed from biblical ethics becomes a cancer on society. Looking at consumer debt today, I can believe it.

QUESTION:

What's the secret for staying out of debt? We are almost out of debt, and I want to make sure we stay out. I fear that once the pressure is off we may go back to spending.

ANSWER:

The only way you're going to solve the debt problem is through personal discipline. Let me give you an idea of a plan that has worked for many people. Fill out an Impulse Buying Sheet that will control all nonbudget spending.

These are the rules. For anything you want to buy that isn't already in your budget and costs more than $10, you get three additional prices and wait thirty days before you buy it (or whatever period of time feels comfortable to you). That will give you time to shop for a better price, and often it allows enough time for that impulse to pass. As soon as the impulse passes, you probably won't even buy that item.

What's happens in many situations is that couples slip into a habit of living beyond their means, so they overspend, go on a crash budget, then overspend again because they're tired of the crash budget. Crash budgets, like crash diets, seldom work. Balance and moderation usually do. The only way to break this cycle is through self-discipline. There is no secret to it.

QUESTION:

Since we owe so much, we can't pay on every bill. What are our options?

Most of our debt is in credit cards—about $15,000—but we're also behind in our equity loan and two car payments. Do you think that we should try for another equity loan or refinance all of our debt to try to get caught up?

ANSWER:

The important thing to remember (and something I can't stress enough) is that debt is a *symptom*. The amount of money you owe is a symptom, not a problem. The symptom will keep returning if you don't correct the problem. If I'm counseling people who have the symptom of too much debt and they're thinking about consolidating, my prerequisite is for them to live six months with no new credit and charge nothing whatsoever.

Commit to a very strict budget so you know where your money is going and exactly how much you can pay your creditors. Then I suggest that you work through one of the credit management organizations, like Consumer Credit Counseling Services (you'll find their number and Web site at the end of this chapter). They will negotiate with the creditors to reduce the interest rates and alter the payments to fit your budget.

I would not recommend consolidating the loans again—at least not until you have been on a budget a minimum of six to nine months or, even better, a year. You need to demonstrate self-discipline first. *"Like a city that is broken into and without walls is a man who has no control over his spirit"* (Proverbs 25:28).

The common question is, "Well, what do we do if we have an emergency—like the tires wearing out or the car breaking down?" The answer is that you need to pray, trust the Lord, and learn to do without until you can commit to no more borrowing. Until you do, you will never solve this problem.

It's important to understand why the debt occurred in the first place. Many people say, "Well, I lost my job," or "My wife got sick," but remember, there are hundreds of thousands of other couples out there who lose their jobs or their spouses get sick, and they don't go into debt. Some of them have families or friends who help, and others simply do without rather than overspend. So it's important to *solve the problem*, which usually is a violation of the basic biblical principles for handling money.

Question:
Where do we start when we owe so much?

We have about $25,000 in credit card debt, and we make about $50,000 a year, but we never seem to get ahead, and we argue all the time. I feel like my husband won't face reality, but he says that he has tried budgeting before and it doesn't work and, besides that, he can't be bothered with these things because he has to earn a living. I tried to get us on a budget, but we have two car payments and a house payment, and we are saving nothing toward retirement.

Answer:
First, you need to pray together about this problem. There's no way you're going to solve this situation unless both of you work on it together. I suggest that you sit down together and list all the debts. Do not exclude anything, including old debts that you haven't paid on, family loans, everything.

If you can't do that without fighting, my recommendation is to schedule an appointment with a marriage counselor. Ask your pastor if there is someone in the church who can work with you.

If not, Crown has several thousand trained financial counselors around the country.

If you're serious about getting yourselves out of debt, keep a diary of what you're spending, by category (Housing, Auto, Food, Clothing, and so forth), for at least one month. A lot of your monthly income can be consumed in the variable expenses that don't necessarily show up in your checkbook every month (miscellaneous items).

You also have to face reality: One of your cars, perhaps even your home, are all luxuries; they are not necessities. Until you're willing to face the reality that some of those don't fit your income, your budget isn't going to work.

Then, together, you need to make out a budget. It probably won't work the first month. It may not work the first five or six months; but, if you'll stick to it, it will be working a year from the time you started. Initially, some categories—like Automobile(s), Entertainment (vacations) and Miscellaneous (gifts, haircuts, and so on)—won't have money in them.

It may mean relying on the help of friends, family—even your church. This is where many people fail—because of pride. The thing I try to remind people of in this situation is that others will help if you'll just ask. If you would help a friend in your situation (and most would), others will too. *"Take hold of instruction; do not let go. Guard her, for she is your life"* (Proverbs 4:13).

QUESTION:
How do we pay off our debt?

Even though we owe a lot, we think that it's within our income ability to pay it. We have a good income and we do have some surplus now, but where should we start? Is it better to invest some of the money for the long term or to pay off all our debt?

Answer:

I wouldn't worry about long-term investing at this point. One of the principles I share is to never do one thing to the exclusion of everything else. First, if you don't have any personal savings, I recommend that you take some of the surplus and set it aside for emergencies—the amount depends on your income. I'd say that if you have a $50,000 income, you should set aside $4,000 or $5,000 in a cash reserve. That way you're not dependent on credit anymore; you can rely on your own money.

But other than that, it's preferable to pay off your debts before any long-term investing. Outlined below, you'll find a debt elimination strategy than can also be used for credit payoff. I recommend that you pay on the high-interest loans first; however, there are some exceptions. If you have several small bills, even at lower interest rates, it may be better to concentrate on paying those. It's encouraging to see some of the bills being paid off, and it allows more money to pay on the other debts. Of course, any plan for reducing debt requires that no more debt be incurred. The following method can be used for eliminating debt, including credit card payoff.

Debt Elimination Strategy (example)

Acct Name	Monthly Payment	Interest Rate	Balance Due
#1	$50	18.2 %	$1,500
#2	$50	18.6 %	$ 860
#3	$50	21.8 %	$ 475
#4	$100	23.2 %	$ 690

> Organize the list (as much as possible) with largest balances toward the top (#1) and smallest balances toward the bottom (#4). Do your best to list accounts with the highest interest rates toward the bottom of the list. Concentrate on paying off the account at the bottom of the list first, and systematically work your way to the top. When a debt is paid, apply the amount you had been paying for that one to the next higher debt.

Another thing to keep in mind is, don't sacrifice everything else in your budget. For instance, don't totally eliminate your Entertainment/Recreation budget (or your travel budget) or your Clothing budget. You need to maintain a reasonable balance in each category.

"Be strong, and let your heart take courage" (Psalm 27:14). You didn't get into this situation overnight, and you're not going to get out of it overnight; therefore, you need to have a balanced perspective toward budgeting. Write down your goals, when you want to achieve them, and then review them about every six months to remind yourself why you're doing this.

QUESTION:

Can companies that advertise they can fix bad credit reports actually do it?

I have a bad credit report, and when we applied for a home mortgage loan we were turned down. My credit report shows several slow pays and two no pays. They are accurate, but I would like to know how to fix my credit report. Is that possible?

ANSWER:

Remember this: When a deal sounds too good to be true, it generally is. And this deal sounds too good. There is basically no way to fix your credit report, except to pay the bills and get a note or a let-ter from the satisfied creditor, which is attached to your credit report. I know of no other way except to wait for the reporting statute to expire. Generally speaking, bad credit reports (with the exceptions of bankruptcies and a couple of others) will be reported for seven years.

Bankruptcies can be reported for up to ten years, at which time they must be removed. But again, the best way to clear up your account is to pay the money you owe and then ask your creditors to notify the credit reporting agencies. One notification should come to you and one to the credit reporting agency. If the information doesn't get into your account, you should contact the credit reporting agencies. You'll find a list of them and their Web sites at the end of this chapter.

The bottom line is that, essentially, you need to reestablish good credit by paying your bills. There's no company out there that can do that for you. All they can do is take your money.

QUESTION:
What does the term "surety" mean?

I've heard you use the term often in discussing finances.

ANSWER:
God's Word says, *"He who is guarantor* [surety] *for a stranger will surely suffer for it, but he who hates being a guarantor is secure"* (Proverbs 11:15). Surety means personally guaranteeing an obligation. Co-signing a note for another person is an example of surety. When somebody borrows money and you sign the note, if that person doesn't pay, you have to. That's called surety.

Almost everybody who borrows money today signs surety. For

instance, if you borrow on an automobile, you sign surety. The lender knows that the automobile is rarely worth what you owe on it, so the loan agreement guarantees any deficiency if you have to sell the car or give it back to the lender. Thus, you are in surety.

About the only way you can avoid surety is to have collateral that can be surrendered in total payment of a debt. For instance, if you borrowed to buy a piece of land that cost $100,000, and you put down $10,000, an exculpatory contract (nonsurety) would stipulate, "If I can't pay for this, I'll let you keep the money I paid in, give you the land back, and be free and clear from all liability." In my opinion, that's the only way you can absolutely avoid surety.

QUESTION:
What is overdraft protection?

We've just opened our first checking account and our banker offered a service called automatic overdraft protection. He said that if we ever overdraw our checking account, the bank will cover the deficiency. Sounds like a good idea to me, but I know it must have some drawbacks.

ANSWER:
In my opinion, automatic overdraft protection presents two distinct dangers. Number one, it encourages people not to keep their checking accounts balanced, because they know they have this overdraft protection. And, number two, an overdraft is an automatic loan. It comes out of a credit account, and you're going to be charged a fee plus interest in most banks for using it.

I believe the automatic overdraft is one of the worst banking services ever offered and one of the quickest sources of debt for undisciplined couples who don't balance their checkbooks. *"Understanding is a fountain of life to him who has it, but the discipline of fools is folly"* (Proverbs 16:22).

QUESTION:

Do you think the Bible teaches that we shouldn't borrow money?

I found a passage in Romans 13:8 that says, *"Owe nothing to anyone except to love one another; for he who loves his neighbor has fulfilled the law."*

ANSWER:

To interpret Romans 13:8 correctly, you must read Romans 13:1–7. It's my opinion that the apostle Paul was not referring to money in the verse you mentioned. He was literally saying, "Don't let anyone do something for you unless you are willing to do more for them."

If Paul had been telling us that Christians should never borrow money, he would have made it absolutely clear and would have clarified that in many other places, which he did not do. Paul would not have relied on a single Scripture verse to overturn all the teaching in God's Word covering the subject of debt. The Old Testament (which was Paul's only testament) has dozens of references to the dangers of debt, the advantages of not having debt, and how to pay debt. After much review, I have concluded that Paul was not referencing money in this particular passage.

QUESTION:

Should we get a fixed loan for our thirty-year mortgage, or is an adjustable rate mortgage better?

ANSWER:

The key principle of an adjustable rate mortgage (ARM) is that it is adjustable; it can go down, but it also can go up. If you get an ARM at a lower rate than a fixed rate loan, you need to make absolutely sure that you can make the maximum payment, if you have to. Logically, if the fixed rate loan is about 2 percent higher than the ARM and the ARM can only increase by 2.5 percent, then the most you would have to risk is one-half of 1 percent, and it's probably worth that risk.

However, many couples have taken on ARMs that don't have caps, and some of these mortgages can go up 4, 5, even 6 percent or more. In my opinion, they are ticking time bombs. I recommend that when rates are down ARM loans be converted as quickly as possible to either a fixed rate loan or at least an ARM with a cap.

"A prudent man sees evil and hides himself; the naive proceed and pay the penalty" (Proverbs 27:12).

QUESTION:

Could you give us your opinion of credit cards?

We were recently married, and we continually get credit card applications mailed to us. I would like to have one, but my husband says that credit cards are evil and that a Christian shouldn't borrow money and, therefore, we can't use credit cards.

ANSWER:

As far as I know, credit cards are not biblically prohibited; nor are they evil. The problem is not credit cards; the problem is the misuse of credit cards.

The problem starts when children see their parents using credit cards to buy everything. As a consequence, when they have the ability to get their own credit cards, they use them to buy things they can't afford. I personally find that even though credit cards are not essential, they are a great convenience.

Let me give you and your husband some simple guidelines that will help you avoid credit card difficulty. Ask your husband to read this, then pray about it, and try to reach a more balanced perspective.

First, you should live on a budget and the two of you should make a simple vow never to use your credit cards to buy anything that is not in your budget that month.

Second, pay the balance you owe on your credit cards every month, with no exception. This means you will never pay any interest.

And third, the first month you aren't able to pay off your credit cards, destroy them. If you'll do this, you won't have a problem with credit cards, but you can enjoy their convenience.

QUESTION:

If I owe $200 per month on my car but I can afford the payments, is this considered debt?

ANSWER:

Well, unfortunately it's not so simple to define what debt is or is not. In our generation, when you borrow money, people say that you're in debt. But if you're able to make the payments, you really aren't in debt; what you have is an obligation to pay. Unfortunately, a great many Americans qualify as being in debt, because they aren't able to make all the monthly payments on the money they have borrowed.

In my opinion, *debt* should be defined as "an obligation to pay without the ability to meet the payments."

"To a person who is good in His sight He has given wisdom and knowledge and joy" (Ecclesiastes 2:26).

QUESTION:
Can you tell me something about student loans?

My husband and I both have student loans. I have been paying on mine regularly since I graduated and they are down to where they'll be paid off in about two years; it will have taken me just under ten years to pay them off. My husband, who graduated the same year I did, still owes about 75 percent of his student loans. He's been very erratic in paying, and there are many penalties attached. He thinks that after ten years the statute of limitations has run out, and he no longer owes for his student loans. Is that right?

ANSWER:
Trying to avoid paying a legitimate debt is unbiblical. *"The wicked borrows and does not pay back, but the righteous is gracious and gives"* (Psalm 37:21). God says if you owe money you are to pay it; that's a vow we make as Christians. We are obligated to pay our debts.

Further, as far as I know, there is no statute of limitations on student loans. Not only is there no statute of limitations, but also you can't go bankrupt to avoid repaying a student loan. Therefore, he's going to have to pay the money back, and the interest can compound greatly.

Recently I had a caller on the program who started with a $25,000 student loan, failed to meet the minimum payments of the loan for about fifteen years, and now owes almost $90,000 on the $25,000 debt.

So my advice is to pay it. Work out a payment plan and meet the payment schedule. You cannot avoid it; nor should you.

QUESTION:

What are my options in paying off a student loan that I have had for almost five years?

I looked at the amortization schedule they sent me, and I was aghast that I had only paid a small amount of principal on this loan. If I continue to pay on it at this rate, it is going to take me the better part of thirty years to pay off my veterinary school debt of about $140,000.

ANSWER:

There is a way to pay it off sooner, but it requires both discipline and sacrifice. Yours is a simple interest loan, meaning that the interest is calculated on the unpaid balance each month. I recommend that you make your regular payment, the minimum amount that is required, and then make an additional payment each month.

Further, commit that, from this point forward, 50 percent of all additional monies that come in—whether from fees you earn at the clinic, gifts of money, an inheritance, or whatever the source—will be used to pay off your student loans. By doing this, you'll pay them off much sooner and save yourself a lot of interest. Do not string out this debt for thirty years.

QUESTION:

Do you think it would be better for us to pay off our undergraduate school loans before going to graduate school?

My husband and I have about $14,000 in undergraduate school loans still unpaid. We will accumulate about another $60,000 of debt if we go to graduate school.

Answer:

With the exception of a few chosen careers, it will be very difficult, even with both of you working, to repay $75,000 in school loans. What happens if you have children and want to stay home with them? Then you would lose your income and make it even more difficult to pay on the loans.

My personal recommendation would be not to accumulate that much debt. One of you, preferably your husband, should go back to school part-time. Stretch out the education over a longer period of time so that, rather than accumulating so much debt, you accumulate only a minimum amount.

Some graduate schools make provisions for working adults to go part-time, until they have accumulated all but one year of credit hours—then go to school full-time for one year. As a result, that total indebtedness will probably be closer to $10,000 than to $60,000 and will make it much easier to pay back those loans.

Just be very careful about accumulating so much debt. It's very difficult to pay it off. In your case, it would be the equivalent of buying a small home and never being able to live in it—a very tough thing to do.

Question:

Can you help us get out of debt?

We're a young couple, married for nearly two years. We came

into this marriage with debt, and the debt continues to accumulate. Our budget is already very tight, so I'm not sure at this point how we can pay off our bills on a month-by-month basis. I have no idea how to deal with this.

ANSWER:

First and foremost, you and your husband need to get on a budget. You'll find budget information under Additional Resources at the end of Chapter 2. Also, you need to accept the responsibility that you have to manage your money in a biblical fashion, which means you cannot spend more than you make.

You must make whatever sacrifices are necessary to bring the spending level down, and there's only one way to do that: discipline. That means you have to evaluate each category in your budget and compare the guideline with your spending (see the Percentage Guide for Family Income table on page 119. Be sure you're not spending too much on any category. For instance, if you are spending too much on your home and you're more than 10 percent above the suggested percentage, it's very likely you won't be able to balance your budget.

Don't make the mistake of allocating more to Housing and nothing to Clothing or Entertainment, because in reality people do buy clothing and they do take vacations. So, for your budget to work you must allocate a percentage to each category and limit your spending to those percentages. Otherwise, no budget will work.

Remember that God understands what your needs are and He will provide. All He requires is that you submit your rights to Him. If you find yourself worried and distressed over this, turn it over to God. "[Cast] *all your anxiety upon Him, because He cares for you"* (1 Peter 5:7).

ADDITIONAL RESOURCES

If you want to investigate working through a credit management organization, we recommend one like Consumer Credit Counseling Services at (800) 251-CCCS or Web site www.cccsatl.org.

The Federal government has laws designed to protect consumers. For information about the Consumer Credit Protection Act, go to their Web site, www.ftc.gov/bcp/menu-credit.htm.

For information about any of the three credit reporting agencies and your credit report, you can contact them at:

- Equifax; P.O. Box 740241 Atlanta, GA 30374-0241; (800) 685-1111; www.equifax.com
- Experian; (formerly TRW) P.O. Box 949 Allen, TX 75013; (888) EXPERIAN (397-3742); www.experian.com
- Trans Union; 760 West Sproul Rd.; P.O. Box 390 Springfield, PA 19064-0390; (800) 916-8800; www.tuc.com

The Fair Debt Collection Practices Act (TFDCPA) was passed by Congress in 1977. The law does not erase any legitimate debt you owe; however, the act prohibits certain debt collection practices.

For a more detailed description of the TFDCPA, get a copy of *Debt-Free Living* at your local Christian bookstore or by calling (800) 722-1976. Also, go to www.ftc.gov/os/statutes/fdcpajump.htm.

The following Internet sites provide helpful financial aid information for financing your education:

- www.collegeboard.org
- www.collegenet.com
- www.embark.com
- www.salliemae.com
- www.collegequest.com

For a copy of the U.S. Department of Education's FAFSA form (Free Application for Federal Student Aid), go to their Internet site, www.fafsa.ed.gov, or call (800) 4-FEDAID.

Gordon Wadsworth's book, *Cost Effective College*, www.costeffectivecollege.com, has strategies and resources to help students pay for the high cost of college whether it's tomorrow or years from now. It has hands-on advice on things such as lists of Internet sites that offer free scholarship services, samples of Free Application for Federal Student Aid (FAFSA) forms, ways to maximize your acceptance at the colleges of your choice, and how to turn college loans into grants upon graduation.

Murray Baker is the author of *The Debt-Free Graduate: How to Survive College Without Going Broke,* www.debtfreegrad.com. To order a copy of the book, call Crown Financial Ministries at (800) 722-1976 or visit your local Christian bookstore.

Dan Cassidy is the author of *Last Minute College Financing, Dan Cassidy's Worldwide College Scholarship Directory,* and *The Scholarship Book 2001.* Contact (800) HEADSTART to reach his fee-based search organization, National Scholarship Research Service.

5

GIVING

ouldn't it be great to see God's people open their hearts and give the way they should? We have enough money in North America to fund all the Christian work in the world if the people would just give.

Giving should be an outward, material expression of a deep spiritual commitment, an indication of a willing and obedient heart. We should give out of grateful hearts in an attitude of joy. Sacrificial giving is a way to honor God, but it should be the result of a good attitude.

There are wrong motives for giving: fear (that God will punish you if you don't give) and giving to impress others (giving should be done modestly and humbly—we are not to draw attention to ourselves when we give).

Being doers of the Word and not hearers only is solidified through our giving to God. Regardless of the work to which we're called, few Christians really cannot afford to give, and when giving is done in love it exemplifies the greatest sacrifice ever made for mankind—the death of Jesus on the cross.

Question:
What should I do about tithing?

We owe too much money to be able to tithe, but we would really like to be able to give to God. Should we stop paying our creditors to give to God?

Answer:
My suggestion is to trust God and give what He tells you to give in His Word. If people waited until they were out of debt to tithe, most American Christians would never tithe.

If you have a commitment to your creditors, you have an obligation to do what you've promised. God is not an accountant, but He says that we should always pay our vows.

"It is better that you should not vow than that you should vow and not pay" (Ecclesiastes 5:5).

So, if you can't pay your creditors and also give to God, you should pay your creditors and honor that commitment. In most instances you can do both, but it means making sacrifices. Believe that God will provide what you need if you make the commitment to do it. The word *believe* means to make it a reality in your life.

There is a caveat that I must add: If you are married to an unsaved person who does not see the necessity or does not have the will to give, in my opinion you need to let the Lord guide you. That doesn't mean not to give, but it also means don't drive a wedge between you and your spouse or a potential wedge between your spouse and the Lord. It would be better to start off giving a small amount and let God convict your spouse than it would be to start off with a large amount, not be able to pay your creditors, and alienate your spouse.

Remember, giving is an outside expression of an inside conviction. God blesses the heart attitude more than the dollars given. It has been my scriptural and personal observation that the giving habits of individuals usually are direct reflections of their value systems.

Those who sincerely care about the needs of others give, according to their means, to help alleviate those needs. They are the "doers" as described in James: *"Prove yourselves doers of the word, and not merely hearers who delude themselves"* (James 1:22). Those who say they care but fail to back up their words with their money are the "hearers" who delude themselves.

To be sure, we have frauds, phonies, and the lazy in our society who make it easy not to give, on the premise that there are frauds, phonies, and lazy people sopping up charity and tax dollars. But with a little effort you can locate the truly needy who do the best they can and still come up short.

They are the single moms who work three jobs to keep their families fed and housed. They are the families of Chinese Christians who are in prison simply because they believe in Jesus Christ. Or they may be the thousands of kids on the streets of Delhi or the garbage dumps of Juarez, where they eat other people's discards.

One day we'll all stand before our Lord and give an accounting of our lives: *"They were judged, every one of them according to their deeds"* (Revelation 20:13). What we do for the Lord is important. There is an adage that says, "Actions speak louder than words." That is absolutely true when it comes to giving.

John tells us to love not only with words but in truth and with deeds (giving). We are admonished that *"whoever has the world's goods, and sees his brother in need and closes his heart against him, how does the love of God abide in him? . . . Let us not love with word or with tongue, but in deed and truth"* (1 John 3:17–18).

QUESTION:
How much is a tithe, and should we tithe on our net or gross? I have a friend who says that the tithe is not applicable to New Testament Christians—that it is a Jewish law, not a New Testament principle. Is that true?

ANSWER:
The word *tithe* or *zela* means "one-tenth"; therefore, when you see the word *tithe* used in reference to giving, God is saying that He wants His people to give a minimum of one-tenth. The tithe was not a law in the Old Testament; there was no punishment for not tithing.

Think of it this way: Suppose you know there's a law that says you cannot drive through a red light, but you drive through one anyway. A police officer stops you and asks, "Did you know that you drove through that red light?"

You answer, "Yes."

He says, "Okay, just wanted to let you know about it," and he drives off.

If there's no punishment, that really isn't a law. And there was no punishment for not tithing. However, there is a consequence. *"You are cursed with a curse, for you are robbing Me!"* (Malachi 3:9).

In my opinion, the Word teaches that we are to give from our gross personal income. God says, *"Honor the LORD from your wealth, and from the first of all your produce"* (Proverbs 3:9).

I believe that *"from the first"* means that we are to give from our gross income. But remember to do what God convicts you to do, not what anyone else says.

Don't get hung up with rules. *"It is acceptable according to what a man has, not according to what he does not have"* (2 Corinthians 8:12). Give freely what He tells you to give, and He will bless your life.

QUESTION:

Could I take money from my tithe to help my elderly mother, who is in great need? We really don't have a lot of surplus money.

ANSWER:

Yes, I believe you can. However, you should do so only if there are absolutely no other funds from which you can help her. Rarely is that true. What it might mean is that you will have to change your habits or your desires.

"Honor your father and mother . . . that it may be well with you, and that you may live long on the earth" (Ephesians 6:2–3). We are told to honor our fathers and our mothers, so if you have no other funds available from which you can help your family, I believe that God would have no difficulty with you helping them from your tithes or offerings. It's something you need to pray about to get direction from Him.

QUESTION:

Will I be denying God if I don't give to the Lord's work?

I'm married to a really good man who is not a Christian. I'd like to be able to give to the Lord's work, but he doesn't want me to. In fact, our only arguments are about giving. And, if I decide to give, should it come from my income only and not from his?

Answer:

God's Word says, *"Wives, be subject to your husbands, as is fitting in the Lord"* (Colossians 3:18). If your husband is not a believer and doesn't want to give, in my opinion, you should not give against his will.

I encourage every Christian woman to do this: Challenge your husband with Malachi 3:10: *"Bring the whole tithe into the storehouse, so that there may be food in My house, and test Me now in this . . . if I will not open for you the windows of heaven, and pour out for you a blessing until it overflows."* Then ask him if you can give a small amount of money, with the agreement that you'll give for one year, and if you're worse off financially at the end of that year's time you'll cease giving. But indicate that if you're better off financially, you would like to be able to give some more.

This is one area (tithing) in God's Word where he says to test Him and trust Him. He promises to prove Himself true. On a personal note, I have seen God do it many times. If you honor your husband and agree with him on what you're doing, God will bless you. He does not want the tithe to cause separation between any husband and wife.

Another word of caution about your incomes. Don't categorize them as "my income" and "his income." When you begin to split incomes, you begin to split families. Instead, make the commitment that it is all "our income." It is all from the Lord and not from you or your husband, so you should treat it that way.

QUESTION:

Is it acceptable for me to give time rather than money?

We are really tight on money, and I have decided to volunteer time to my church rather than to give tithes. My wife disagrees with this, and she says that she thinks we are to give money and that time is not a good substitute. What do you think?

ANSWER:

I believe that God wants you to give both time and money, so I think that your wife is correct: Time is not a substitute for money. We are instructed by God to give for one reason: as a testimony. I know it's difficult to give time. Many people are more stingy with their time than they are with their money; but, we are to give both, and one is not a substitute for the other.

Your attitude about money is important, and if you learn to budget your money and give, even though things are tight, I believe it will make you a better money manager and, therefore, a better steward. Bottom line, in my interpretation of God's Word, time is not a substitute for money when it comes to giving.

QUESTION:

Should my entire tithe go to my local church?

We're members of an excellent church that is part of a denomination that I strongly disagree with. I think that we should not give our money to our church, since a large portion goes to the denomination; my husband disagrees. What do you think?

ANSWER:

The purpose of the tithe is to help other people. It pays your pastor, it supports mission work through your local church, and it helps the widows and orphans of the Christian and non-Christian community. My counsel is that if you cannot entrust your funds unreservedly to your local church, and therefore to your denomination, then you're probably in the wrong place. Unless you have been called there as a missionary of the Lord, you need to leave this denomination. The Lord may be telling you to move on by creating this lack of peace about where your tithes should go.

QUESTION:

Since we are currently between churches and looking for the one God would have us join, should we give our tithe to the churches we are visiting?

ANSWER:

The Scripture says that we are to support those who teach us. *"The Lord directed those who proclaim the gospel to get their living from the gospel"* (1 Corinthians 9:14). If you're going to a church, even though you aren't a member, and you attend for any substantial period of time, I encourage you to give to that church.

However, you need to be careful where your funds are going and be sure they are being used wisely. That's something you can't discern if you just visit a church one time. One suggestion would be to open a special savings account for the tithes that you're not giving currently. Put your tithes in this account until you're a little bit more settled on a church home.

But be careful. There will be a temptation to dip into those funds for other things, so you need to commit the money for your tithes. There are some community foundations that will allow you to put the money into their foundation and direct where it will go later. These are called self-directed funds. You'll find a reference to some at the end of this chapter.

QUESTION:
What should I do about giving?

I'm a Christian but my wife isn't. I really want to give, but she vehemently disagrees with me and we always end up in an argument.

ANSWER:

According to God's Word, husbands are to be the leaders of their homes, but you shouldn't let your giving cause a rift in your marriage. Make every attempt to share with your wife the biblical truths about tithing and giving. Then challenge her to tithe as a family and see how God will bless you.

But as the authority of your family, even if your wife doesn't agree, you must do what God is telling you to do. This may, in fact, temporarily alienate your wife, but most wives are looking for strong, godly leadership—not a dictator but a leader. And if these principles are real in your life, she will see that tithing is a commitment in your life, not a legalism. Let me encourage you not to force the decision on your wife just to assert your authority. Do your very best to convince her that this is a heartfelt conviction within you.

Pray about this, give it a lot of time and prayer. I believe that God is going to prove Himself through your finances, but ultimately, if you are to be the leader of your home, you have to do what God is convicting you to do. And remember what Jesus told us in Matthew 10:37: *"He who loves father or mother more than Me is not worthy of Me; and he who loves son or daughter more than Me is not worthy of Me."* This is a tough biblical truth, but I believe that God will bless you through it. I have yet to see a marriage dissolve over the husband obeying a conviction from the Lord to give, though I realize it's always possible.

QUESTION:

What do you think about giving a portion of my tithe to the United Way?

I believe that if these organizations are doing the work that God really wants to have done, they are worthy of getting a portion of my tithe; however, my wife strongly disagrees.

ANSWER:

The tithe you give is a portion of your income that has been committed to God and is given as a testimony in God's name. There are many organizations that do great work, but the ministries that serve in God's name, not secular organizations, should be the recipients of our tithes. That doesn't mean that you can't support them, but don't use your tithe to do so.

This is our testimony that God owns everything in our lives, including our finances, and the tithe should not be used to support secular organizations that don't serve in the Lord's name. That does not mean that they are not worthy. It's fine to support them, but do it with your money, not with God's.

QUESTION:

Do you think we should tithe on a gift from my parents?

My husband says that because it isn't income we shouldn't tithe on it. However, I think we ought to tithe on everything that comes in.

ANSWER:

I believe that you're right. God's Word does not tell us to tithe only on earned income. It tells us that we should give from the firstfruits of everything that comes into our possession. But bear in mind that, as I have said before, God is not an accountant, and He's not sitting up there with a ledger book trying to determine whether you have given the right amount of money into His kingdom.

The purpose of the tithe is to act as an outside indicator of an inside spiritual condition. If your husband is not committed to giving and is doing it grudgingly or under compulsion, there really is no reward for doing that. My encouragement to you would be to read Malachi 3:8–10 to your husband and help him understand the purpose of the tithe. Then allow God to convict him about what he should do.

QUESTION:

Should we stop tithing until we pay off our debts?

My husband says that he thinks we should stop tithing because we owe so much money in credit cards and other debt. I don't think that we should do this; however, he says that it is a better testimony to pay our creditors than it is to give to God while we owe so many people. What do you think?

ANSWER:

To some degree I think that both of you are correct. It is not a good testimony to owe people money and not be paying them. However, in my opinion, it also is not a good testimony to claim that we belong to God and that Christ is first in our lives and then not be willing to give from our material assets as evidence of that.

If you can make the minimum payments on your debt, even if it requires working through one of the credit consolidators, it would be better to pay the minimum amount and give God the tithe than it would be to pay more than the minimum amount and not give the tithe.

QUESTION:

What should my attitude be about the church taking up an offering at every service?

I find myself getting resentful when I see the offering plate going around. It's like the church is begging us to give to them, and I wonder how offensive this is to our visitors and perhaps to the non-Christians who are in our congregation.

ANSWER:

Scripture doesn't dictate how an offering should be collected. I've been in churches that put an offering box at the back of the church and never ask for money. I've been in churches that passed around a plate. And I've been in other churches where the pastor would cajole his people into giving more.

Other than from a personal perspective, I don't know that one is more right than the other. The apostle Paul tells us about giving in church: *"Now concerning the collection for the saints, as I directed the churches of Galatia, so do you also. On the first day of every week, let each one of you put aside and save, as he may prosper, that no collections be made when I come"* (1 Corinthians 16:1–2).

The first day of the week for us is Sunday, as it was in the apostle Paul's time, so what he was saying to them was, put aside some money so I don't have to gather this offering when I come.

If I were a pastor, I would try not to offend people, but I would do what I believed was right. I don't think passing around an offering plate is wrong; nor do I think it's begging. It's interesting to me that we will give to a variety of causes whose representatives call us on the telephone or come to our doors—everything from supporting our local fire department and police department to collecting money for muscular dystrophy—but somehow we think it's wrong for God's people to ask to keep the church going. I don't feel that way.

I would suggest that your motive may be wrong. Test your motive and see if it's the giving you object to or the passing of the plate.

Question:

Do you have any guidelines for giving?

I have difficulty with so many groups always asking for money. I'm sure many of them are doing good work, but I don't know where I should give.

Answer:

First and foremost, you need to pray and be sure that wherever you're giving, it's where you believe God wants you to give. But when you are testing an organization, first get some information from them to find out how much of their money they spend in fund-raising versus programs. If more than about 25 percent goes to fund-raising, in my opinion, the organization is out of balance. Too much of your money is going to raise more money.

Second, do you know that the organization teaches a message that is true to God's Word, and are people responding by either accepting Christ or becoming better disciples of Christ? Are the lives of the leaders of this organization consistent with Christian principles? And is the organization multiplying itself through the teaching of God's Word?

I realize it's difficult to ascertain this information, particularly when you're talking about just giving $10 to an organization that comes door-to-door. Personally, what I would do is get the Form 990, which tells where their money goes every year. I would try to get some literature from the organization and find out what they stand for, and I also would pray about it. If you're considering giving any sizable amount of money, I probably would go visit the organization personally. You want to be the best steward of what God has given to you.

QUESTION:
Wouldn't it be better if I contributed directly to needy people rather than going through a church or some other organization?

I've really been turned off by so many ministries soliciting money, supposedly to help the poor, but I suspect that much of my money is going into buildings and travel and other overhead.

ANSWER:

Sometimes it's proper and better to give to an individual, particularly if you're trying to reach somebody in your own community or perhaps even in your own neighborhood. In fact, I've often suggested to people to find a single mother in their church to help. If they do and she's the average single mother, they'll be helping a needy person.

But what about the people who aren't in your community or your local church? What about people who live in other countries who are needy? Without distribution organizations, we would never be able to meet their needs. Number one, you probably couldn't go to the country; number two, you couldn't get through the political system to bring anything into the country; and number three, you wouldn't know who is needy and who is not. So there's a legitimate purpose for these organizations.

Giving is the true evidence of caring. *"Whoever has the world's goods, and sees his brother in need and closes his heart against him, how does the love of God abide in him?"* (1 John 3:17).

I do recommend that if you are giving to someone, do not give cash. You might help buy food, pay rent, pay a utility bill, or something else, but unless you're well trained in how to counsel people and determine if the money is being used properly, you might just be adding to somebody else's weakness. That's particularly true when you give to beggars on the street. You may think that you are feeding them, but in fact you may just be feeding a very bad habit. Well-organized charities do a much better job of sorting out the needy from the greedy than most individuals can.

ADDITIONAL RESOURCES

The National Christian Foundation focuses on providing an opportunity, vehicle, and procedure for people to give, in the areas that God has encouraged and equipped them to give, through donor-advised funds.

National Christian Foundation
1100 Johnson Ferry Rd. NE, Ste. 900
Atlanta, GA 30342
Phone: (404) 252-0100
Fax: (404) 252-5277

The Foundation Center has libraries in several cities around the U.S. and provides many publications and services that can help you find a Christian or community foundation through which you may give donor-advised gifts.

The Foundation Center
79 Fifth Ave. at 16th St.
New York, NY 10003-3076
Tel: (212) 620-4230 *or* (800) 424-9836
Fax: (212) 807-3677
Internet: www.fdncenter.org

6

INSURANCE

*T*he area of insurance has gotten increasingly confusing for most people. That's hardly surprising since there are so many different types of insurance that come in an almost infinite variety of options. If you can say it, there's an insurance company out there somewhere that will write a policy to cover it.

Wow! Things used to be a lot simpler back when doctors made home visits, babies were birthed by midwives, and Uncle Charlie fashioned Uncle Bob's coffin in his carpentry shop.

I hope this section will help sort out some of the most commonly asked questions about insurance for you.

QUESTION:
Can you give me some information about life insurance? I don't know what type of insurance is best for us; I'm confused about buying whole life insurance versus term insurance.

ANSWER:

Buying life insurance depends on your age, health, and how much money you have in your budget to spend on it. *Term insurance* is usually the cheapest in the short term. You buy term insurance for a determinable period of time—perhaps for one year, five years, ten years, or twenty years—hence the name "term." The cost of any life insurance is going to depend on two things: your age and how long you'll need the insurance.

Term insurance is the least expensive and the most common kind of insurance available. However, the longer you keep term, the costlier it gets. One of the arguments for buying *term* insurance is that you can buy the cheapest insurance and invest the difference elsewhere—typically mutual funds, or the like, that will accumulate more money over the long run. When you look at it financially, that argument seems to be true; but, in practical fact, the majority of people don't get around to investing the difference in the money. They usually spend it.

Conversely, when you buy *cash value* insurance you pay a fixed price per month for the duration of the contract period—often the rest of your life. Obviously, because they are insuring you over a much longer period of time, the insurance companies are going to charge more for the policy up front. Then the companies take a portion of that premium overcharge and the accumulating cash value to offset the company's increasing liability as you get older.

Common sense says that a thirty-year-old is at less risk of dying than a sixty-year-old. Therefore the company overcharges the younger person and keeps part of that money in reserve, so that when the insured is sixty years old the company can offset some of its risk. That's the basic difference between *term* and *cash value*. It's not that one is more or less costly; they average out essentially the same over your lifetime. The only difference is that at a younger age you can afford more *term*, which is when most people need the maximum amount of insurance.

Bear in mind that, with few exceptions, most of the cash in your *cash value* policy belongs to the insurance company and not to you. There are some very good policies—both *term* and *cash value*—now available. Some *cash value* policies invest in mutual funds and other investments that help offset the increasing cost of the premium. Some will return a portion of the accumulated cash or dividends to the insured.

Let me make it clear that no one insurance plan fits everybody. *Term* insurance is great for younger couples and people who have a short-term need, and I heartily recommend it. Usually the maximum amount of insurance is needed during the most critical years of your life: generally when you're a young family with children. As you get older, the *term* insurance is going to get decidedly more expensive, and you can drop some of it. So my advice about buying insurance is to shop, shop, shop.

The majority of people do need some kind of permanent insurance, but as they get older the tendency is to drop the *term* and carry no insurance, which is not a good idea. I also recommend that you avoid buying life insurance, or any other financial product, from a part-time salesperson. Stick with a professional—someone who is in the business to make a living from it. The reason I say that is because I have seen many part-time people who've sold insurance, investments, and other financial products and then went on their way, and the people they insured were left with nobody to follow up later. You'll get a lot better service if you buy from a professional, even if you have to pay a little more in terms of commission.

QUESTION:
What are my options for health insurance now that I've lost my job? I won't have any insurance when I leave this company.

ANSWER:
There are only a few options available to most people. Under the COBRA Act, you can continue the insurance that your company offers (if they have twenty or more employees). However, you probably will pay the total cost of the insurance—the employee's portion and the company's portion, plus a small administrative fee. In general, it's about 103 percent of the total cost.

I would use that provision only if you have a preexisting condition that precludes you from getting insurance elsewhere. Usually, the coverage in a company's group plan is better than what you can buy on your own, but most people don't need that kind of coverage. More commonly, what you need is a higher-deductible disaster insurance—in other words, a major medical insurance plan with a $500 to $1,000 deductible.

There are some alternative plans available that are called *share cost* plans. In other words, you pool your money with other people and the accumulated surplus provides for the major costs of the members of the plan. You'll find these advertised in many Christian magazines, and that principle is discussed in God's Word: *"At this present time your abundance being a supply for their need that their abundance also may become a supply for your need, that there may be equality"* (2 Corinthians 8:14). However, you need to investigate thoroughly the extent of what the plans cover and what they do not.

Additionally, some states have state insurance health plans for those who have been turned down for health insurance—for whatever reason.

Unfortunately, the bottom line is that there are no real bargains in health insurance these days.

QUESTION:
Do I really need the group disability insurance my company offers?

ANSWER:
In my opinion, a group disability through an employer is one of the best bargains available in insurance. You do need to review the plan carefully, though, because there are many different options in any disability plan. Choose those that fit your need.

Some plans are short-term and will cover you until you're qualified for Social Security disability, some will cover you only for a few months, and some will cover you for the rest of your life. The cost of each is different, so you need to read the policies and buy only what you need.

In my opinion, disability insurance is not one of those critical areas of insurance. First, I would provide for life and health insurance, and then, if you can afford it within your budget, decide on disability. Many professionals—doctors, lawyers, pilots, dentists—often will carry disability plans so that if they can't practice their profession for whatever reason (usually health reasons), their incomes are protected. Many of those plans are very comprehensive but also very expensive.

Individually purchased disability policies are usually much more expensive than group plans; but, again, dollar for dollar many of those are also good bargains. In my opinion, if you have enough money in your budget to provide for your life and health insurance needs and a good disability is available through your employer, you should take advantage of it.

QUESTION:
What are our options for health insurance?

My husband is leaving the company he has been with for five years to go into his own business. We are losing access to our 401(k) plan, and we are going to lose our health insurance.

ANSWER:
Under what is called the COBRA Act, your husband can continue his insurance for up to eighteen months. However, in order to do so, you'll have to pay the full cost of the insurance, plus a small premium. That means you'll pay whatever the company is paying for it plus about a 3 to 5 percent handling fee for the insurance, and that can be quite expensive.

I would say that most company policies will cost between $600 and $800 per month. The other option you have is to find private insurance, which is going to be very expensive, or perhaps look into a Christian medical-cost sharing plan, which is often advertised in Christian magazines. Crown Financial Ministries does not endorse these plans, but they may offer reasonable "coverage" for some individuals or couples who cannot afford traditional health insurance. You need to investigate thoroughly what the plans cover and what they do not, any waiting period for preexisting conditions, the monthly cost, and *especially* the average length of time it takes to receive benefits.

As far as your 401(k), that money is still yours. It depends on the contract with the company whether you can leave your 401(k) there. But you can always transfer it to an IRA of your own. You can call any mutual fund company or brokerage house, and they will handle that transaction for you at no expense. Just explain what you want to do.

7

INVESTING AND RETIREMENT

The topic of investing is of great interest to millions of people, since much of their long-term savings is tied up in stocks, bonds, land, and other investments. From 1995 until early 2000, it seemed that investing questions dominated my daily call-in broadcast. A lot of people were making record profits in the stock markets and ordinary citizens wanted in on the action.

Then, in 2000, the questions shifted from "How can I get rich in the market?" to "How can we keep what we have?" Why? Because the markets dropped (as markets are prone to do), but the debts of the average family didn't.

Closely tied to investing is retirement. Retirement, as we know it today, is a relatively new idea and an affluent society's invention. The hard laborers have always had to slow down with age, but the phenomenon of young, healthy people kicking back and enjoying the fruits of their labor is only the evidence of a non-biblically based society.

God intends for us to stay active and involved. If you happen to be fortunate enough to have surplus resources, God expects much of them to be put back into His work. If you have the financial wherewithal to retire, then volunteer with a ministry.

Investment and retirement decisions are never easy. But if you will hear and apply God's principles, most of the wrong reasons to invest and retire will be eliminated. The Bible isn't mute on these two topics. Quite the contrary; it is quite vocal.

QUESTION:

I recently left one company for another and my new company offers a 401(k), but they won't allow me to transfer my old 401(k) into their account. What should I do with the money that is in my previous company's 401(k)?

ANSWER:

First, you should verify with your previous employer that you have the right to leave your account there and, if so, for how long. Also, ask what control you have over the money. Otherwise, you'll need to roll it out of that 401(k) into your own IRA account.

Since your new company won't allow you to put that money into their 401(k), you'll need to set up a private IRA. Though IRAs are limited in the amount you can invest in them per year, there is no limit in a rollover IRA, so you can transfer your savings into an account with any financial institution you desire. Any bank, mutual fund, or stock investment company will set up this IRA for you at no cost.

My recommendation is to choose a good mutual fund company

and roll your money into one of their flexible mutual fund accounts. Then you can spread the money out among the variety of funds they offer. These range from the most conservative, which might be their bond funds, to speculative stock funds, if you desire. As I said, any financial institution you select will set up the IRA for you and will transfer the funds into that account. Most companies provide at least a quarterly accounting of your assets.

If I were choosing a company, I would use a neutral source, such as *Money* magazine or *Consumer Reports* magazine, and select one of their top five companies to do the rollover.

QUESTION:

Can you tell me where to find a financial planner who can help us with our long-term goals? And what should we expect to pay?

ANSWER:

At the end of this chapter, you'll find some sources for financial planners. But bear in mind that you need to find a financial planner who fits your personality and what you're trying to accomplish, and be sure to ask the right questions up front.

The first decision you need to make is whether you're looking for a fee-only financial planner (one paid by the hour or by a set fee) or for a commission-based planner (one who earns his or her income as a result of selling products—mutual funds, stocks and bonds, insurance policies).

There's no right or wrong way to bill for financial services. I personally prefer a fee-only planner, because I feel like I have more control when I pay. Some people prefer to have it included in the investments they're buying. Over the long run, you're still going to pay the cost, no matter which way you choose, because that person has to make a living.

In my opinion, when you're looking for a good financial planner you need to look for a person with longevity in that field. My personal criteria is something like this: someone who has been in the financial planning business for ten years or longer, someone who has the right credentials (the CFP, indicating certification, and other credentials that reflect his or her training), and someone with references. When you get the references, make the effort to call no less than five of the planner's previous clients.

When you call, ask very pointed questions: "How did you like the service? Did that person make money or lose money for you? Is he or she readily available? Do you have good communication with this person?" Don't be bashful; ask the right questions. The bottom line is to find a person who will give you good financial advice so that you'll make more money on your money (after his or her fee) than you'd make if you just invested the money yourself in a good CD.

After all, you don't need a financial adviser to help you park the money in a CD or some other fixed income investment. So you need to weigh the planner's credentials and look at his or her results. If the results show that after the planner's fee you made less money than you could make in a CD, go do it yourself.

QUESTION:
Can you tell me under what conditions you would use a Roth IRA versus the regular IRA?

We're planning to start a retirement account, and we're trying to decide whether it's better for us as a young couple to get a regular IRA or a Roth IRA.

ANSWER:

IRAs are attractive savings vehicles, especially for people who don't have an employer-provided, qualified retirement plan. Under current law, to open an IRA, your income has to be $150,000 per year or less. However, there are other types of retirement accounts that are available to self-employed individuals with incomes in excess of $150,000 per year.

Basically the same qualification rules apply for the regular and the Roth IRA. The difference in the two is that in a regular IRA account you're allowed to put in tax-deferred money, meaning you don't have to pay income tax on that money. But, as the account accumulates and, ultimately, when you take it out for retirement, you're going to be taxed at ordinary income rates on withdrawals, regardless of how the money was earned. In other words, even if you invested in the stock market and you had capital gains income, you would still be taxed at ordinary income rates.

The Roth IRA is different because you contribute after-tax money to the account. In other words, money you have already paid income taxes on. The account accumulates over the years (hopefully), and when you withdraw the funds for retirement purposes it is not taxable income.

In my opinion, the Roth IRA is well suited for younger people, and if I were looking for a retirement plan and qualified for an IRA, I personally would use the Roth IRA. Under many conditions I might choose the Roth IRA even as an older person. It would depend on my tax situation and whether I thought my tax structure would be higher or lower after retirement.

If I thought my tax liability was going to be higher at retirement, the Roth IRA would certainly be the way to go. If I thought my liability was going to be substantially less after retirement, the regular IRA might suit me better. As the old saying goes: Pay them (IRS) now or pay them later.

Question:

Should I be contributing to my 401(k) if our budget is extremely tight?

We seem to be borrowing on our credit cards every month just to get by. This is creating a lot of conflict in my marriage, particularly because it may result in my wife going back to work. At the same time, we're putting $300 a month in our 401(k).

Answer:

In general, long-term saving is a very good idea, and I heartily recommend it for the majority of people—but not at the cost of your marriage. There are other things far more important. You need to look carefully at your budget and find a budget counselor. You'll find references for budget counselors at the end of this chapter. You need to get help immediately on this.

Be aware that many marriages, Christian and non-Christian alike, dissolve over financial arguments. In my opinion, if it takes withdrawing the money out of your 401(k)—even with all the penalties—to resolve this crisis, it's worth it to lower the pressure on your marriage. But don't do it until you've met with a counselor and gotten on a budget. Then you can be sure that you're dealing with the problem, not just treating the symptoms.

Stopping your retirement savings for a while will not hurt your long-term plans; dissolving your marriage will.

"Better is a little with the fear of the LORD than great treasure and turmoil with it" (Proverbs 15:16).

QUESTION:
Can you tell us where the best place is to make money on our money?

We've saved some money for our household contingencies. We would like to be making money on that money, but I want it to be absolutely safe. My husband says we should have it in the stock market where it can grow, but I would rather have it in something secure. We have agreed to follow your counsel.

ANSWER:
I also suggest that this money be put in a very safe place. It is not money that's meant to be invested. If you want to take half of it and use it for long-term savings and keep the other half for short-term expenses, that's fine. If it were my own money, I'd put it in a money market account or something equivalent; I wouldn't be taking stock market risks with it. Those funds need to be accessible when breakdowns or emergencies occur.

A good place to keep this kind of savings is in a money market fund offered by one of the large brokerage firms. Generally speaking, a money market account is going to make the maximum amount of interest with a minimum risk, and your first priority is minimum risk. You're looking for a return *of* your money, not the return *on* your money in this particular situation.

QUESTION:

How safe is a money market account?

My brother has recently told me that I should be keeping my spare money in a money market account rather than a savings account at my local bank, but I don't understand money markets.

ANSWER:

A money market account is basically an interest-bearing account in which many people pool their funds, and it is managed by a professional investment company—like a brokerage firm. Money market accounts yield some of the highest interest rates available for on-demand accounts—where the money you have on deposit is available to you, usually on a daily basis.

In general, a money market account is an at-risk investment, meaning that it is not guaranteed by the FDIC or by any government agency. But if you select one of the large brokerage firms, the probability of you getting your money back, in my opinion, is 100 percent. Many of them have billions of dollars in these accounts, which are used by the brokerage houses for internal operations and for investing, and they are very secure.

The brokerage houses keep a large supply of cash on hand to repay these accounts—far more than your bank does to pay your savings account—and generally you earn a higher interest rate.

The majority of the brokerage firms that offer these kinds of accounts also offer government-backed mutual funds, meaning that your money is backed by the U.S. government, but these funds usually don't pay the same rate of return. Also, be aware that some accounts that are called government securities are not actually secured by the government. They are repurchase agreements, meaning that the government securities are owned by the institution and they back your money as collateral, but the government is not actually guaranteeing the money. In my opinion, money market accounts satisfy the requirement of prudent security and they offer total liquidity.

QUESTION:
Could you help me understand what a mutual fund is and what is involved?

My husband would like for us to put our retirement money in mutual funds, but I am not familiar with mutual funds, except by name.

ANSWER:
A mutual fund is an investment in which many people pool their money together to buy different kinds of securities—like stocks or bonds. In essence, it is a large group of people pooling their money into a common account. Then a professional manager uses that money to invest in stocks or bonds, depending on the type of fund.

In my opinion, mutual funds are good investments for low-budget investors, because they provide a lot of diversification (they invest in many different companies) and they provide professional management. However, bear in mind that the same principle of risk and return always applies: If you want a higher return on your money than you can get by leaving it in a CD or a savings account, then you must be willing to assume a higher risk. Mutual funds go up and down with the markets they represent, and you can lose money as well as make money.

So you need to select your particular fund based on your personality and your ability to handle risk. Look at the track records of the mutual funds very carefully. Mutual funds are profit-making entities; therefore, there are certain risks that every investor must assume.

The companies and salespeople who sell mutual funds make their money through a fee system. There are two kinds of fees in mutual funds: the front-load and the no-load mutual fund. The front-load mutual fund basically means that the service charges for handling the funds and the commission to the salesperson are taken out when you buy your shares, so you have less money working for you up front.

The no-load funds don't take those commissions and fees out up front; therefore the costs are amortized over a number of years. In theory, the no-load mutual funds should have higher earnings, because more money is working for you initially. But if you keep a mutual fund for a substantial period of time—typically six years or longer—statistically, there is virtually no difference in performance between a no-load and a front-load mutual fund (at least that's what the experts on both sides tell me).

Many mutual fund companies will give you the flexibility of shifting your investment among different kinds of funds—what they call their family of funds. So you can invest in low-risk funds, high-risk funds, and mid-risk funds, and you can shift your money back and forth—normally, without a fee.

If you're going to buy into mutual funds, I recommend that you first do some reading. You'll find information about some good materials at the end of this chapter. Then, start slowly, don't invest all your money at one time. And, finally, only invest in companies that are secure, have been around for a long time, and have verifiable track records. At least then you'll know the risks you're taking.

Question:
What is your opinion about stock market investing?

I've been investing in the stock market for four or five years, and initially I made a lot of money—on paper at least. However, in recent years I've lost a substantial amount of money. I'm probably even with the market right now. My wife thinks the stock market is gambling and that Christians shouldn't be involved.

Answer:

We are warned in Proverbs about having the wrong attitude toward worldly riches. I believe that the majority of stock market investors need to heed Proverbs 23:4–5: "*Do not weary yourself to gain wealth, cease from your consideration of it. When you set your eyes on it, it is gone. For wealth certainly makes itself wings, like an eagle that flies toward the heavens.*" I believe that a lot of people are involved in get-rich-quick schemes, not legitimate stock market investing.

In general, when you invest in the stock market you're buying equity in companies like IBM, Xerox, General Motors, Microsoft, and Cisco. What you should be doing is buying their stock in anticipation that the company will grow and make a profit in which you will share.

But when speculators buy stocks whose price-to-earnings ratios (price versus earnings) are in the thousands of percent—in other words, the price they pay for the stock is hundreds or thousands of times higher than the annual earnings of the company—they're not buying that stock for the value of the company. They're buying it for the speculative potential of the stock. Literally, they're speculating (gambling) that the price will go up.

"Do not boast about tomorrow, for you do not know what a day may bring forth" (Proverbs 27:1).

Many people did guess right when the market was going up, but they guessed wrong when the market went down. A great many amateur speculators lost money they couldn't afford to lose.

If you're buying stock for the long term and for the earnings the company can generate, in my opinion, that's investing in the stock market. If you're buying it simply because you think the price will go up and you can sell your inflated stock to someone else at a higher price, that's known as the greater-sucker theory.

So, in large part, it's not *where* you invest your money, it's the *attitude* you have about the investment.

Question:

Is it better to pay off the car or invest?

We've paid down a lot of our debts and now I find that, with a raise, we have $500 a month extra. Do you think that we should put it all on our car payment until we pay it off, which would take only about two years, or should we start doing some investing as well?

ANSWER:

Generally speaking, I encourage you not to do one thing to the exclusion of everything else. My recommendation is, rather than trying to put all your surplus on the automobile, that you spread it over your budget a little bit. Maybe allocate $100 to $150 a month to pay off the car, even if it stretches the payoff to three years rather than two.

Allocate some of the money into your Entertainment/ Recreation budget and perhaps some into your Clothing budget. After your budget is working well, then use some of the surplus to invest.

You and your wife should pray about your budget and do what's best for both of you. It may be that she's been feeling too confined; this is an opportunity to loosen up a little bit. Remember, being the best steward does not necessarily mean being the most frugal. *"It is the blessing of the LORD that makes rich, and He adds no sorrow to it"* (Proverbs 10:22).

QUESTION:

How can you give people advice to invest when in fact it is unscriptural?

I've listened to your radio program for a long time, and I've heard you talk to Christians and give them advice about investing. I believe that Christians should not invest or be involved in the investment world, because this promotes greed and covetousness and money is lost that could otherwise be put back into the kingdom.

ANSWER:

I disagree. If Christians are giving what they believe God wants them to give and they still have a surplus of money, then I believe the

Scripture tells us that some of it is to be put aside for future needs. Otherwise, how would the money be available for the projects that God wants done in the future if we don't save for them?

Proverbs 6:6–11 tells us that ants store food during the summer, knowing that the time will come when they will need those resources. The same thing applies to God's people. We also see in the parable of the talents (Matthew 25:14–30) that God wants us to use our mental and financial assets to further the kingdom of God.

But if all God's Word said about investing is to just make it and store it—in other words, "Make all you can and can all you make"—then many of the rich people of the world would be right on target. However, there is a balance, as found in the parable of the rich fool (Luke 12:16–21).

A farmer is an investor. He takes a portion of his crops and he puts it in the ground, caring for it and trusting that it is going to grow into a large harvest. In the story of the rich fool, he had a large harvest, but instead of looking for how he could share his harvest, he decided he would tear down his barns and build larger ones, and God called him a fool.

So somewhere between the ant who stores and the rich fool is the balance that God wants us to have. That does not preclude God's people from being involved with investing. The scriptural justification for investing is to provide for future needs by multiplying surpluses. Some of the legitimate needs for the future are spontaneous giving, education of your children, getting debt free, and retirement—at least slowing down in your older years. That does not make investing wrong; it makes it a balanced part of God's plan for a Christian.

QUESTION:

Should we stretch our budget and join a retirement plan right now?

Our budget is very tight, but my husband's company offers a retirement plan that matches 10 percent of any money we put in it per year.

ANSWER:

I suggest that you start with about 5 percent of your income and take advantage of this retirement plan. It may stretch your budget; but you can do it if you make it a priority. For example, do you know how people are able to pay taxes? They are deducted from their checks before they get them, and the same principle applies here. You make whatever adjustments you have to. Pay yourself first and put money into a long-term investment account—in your case, the investment account is your company retirement plan. It's a very good idea for most families.

Another point to emphasize: Don't treat your retirement account like a savings account and continually dip into it for the things you want. This is a long-term savings—for retirement or, at the very least, for the education of your children.

You should monitor the results of your retirement account each year and determine whether the money is invested properly. Don't take the approach that someone else is smart enough to know how to invest your money. Nobody cares more about your money than you do, and if you ignore it you can lose some or all of it.

"Without faith it is impossible to please Him, for he who comes to God must believe that He is and that He is a rewarder of those who seek Him" (Hebrews 11:6).

Question:
Where's the best place to invest for retirement?

My husband and I are just beginning our working careers, but we are looking for places to invest our retirement income. Over the last couple of years we have put it in the stock market, but now the stock market has taken a significant drop and we have lost nearly half of what we put in our accounts. Should we even worry about something as long-term as retirement?

Answer:
Yes, you do need to invest for the long term. If you're a couple in your mid- to late twenties, you need to look at the long term, and the long term for most people in this country is the stock market. Of course, the market goes up and the market goes down, but over-all it has gone up for more than one hundred years now.

If I were you, I would start my investing program by choosing a good-quality mutual fund, or perhaps more than one, and put my money there. I like mutual funds primarily because they have professional management and they invest in a great variety of companies, so you automatically have diversity. Granted, you may get in at the wrong time and the market will drop, but it will come back as long as the country is prospering, and we are a very prosperous country.

The concept is called *dollar cost averaging*. This means that you put money in when it is high and you put money in when it is low, and overall you are going to get the average value of the stock market. So I encourage you to use mutual funds to start your investment program. And, because of your ages, I would suggest that you look at growth mutual funds. They are a little more volatile, but since you have many years to invest you should do quite well over the long term.

At the end of this chapter, you'll find resource information on retirement. Read it and then make your own choices.

QUESTION:

My wife and I are in our late-twenties; with all the publicity about how underfunded the Social Security system is, how secure is our Social Security income for when we retire?

ANSWER:

The best anyone can do is give you an opinion about the solvency of Social Security. In my opinion, I believe that those who are already qualified for benefits will be protected no matter what. However, the potential financial difficulties of Social Security are pretty significant.

For younger workers entering the system, I don't believe the future of Social Security looks very good. Fewer new workers are contributing to the system, and the recipients are living a lot longer, which causes an acute actuarial problem. Almost certainly, we are going to push the retirement ages back and reduce the benefits once we get well into the twenty-first century. By about 2020 or so, I believe we are going to see the retirement age increased to about seventy and the benefits decreased dramatically. Otherwise, the system is going to run out of money.

So a young couple, even though they are qualified for Social Security, would be wise to build their own retirement account. Common sense tells me that an alternative retirement would be very prudent for anybody entering the system today. God's Word says, *"The mind of the prudent acquires knowledge, and the ear of the wise seeks knowledge"* (Proverbs 18:15).

ADDITIONAL RESOURCES

You can find information on subjects such as mutual funds and the index funds by looking in financial magazines such as *Cheapskate Monthly, Consumer Reports, Family Money, Frugal Living Newsletter, Kiplinger* (which has several specialized magazines), and *Money*. Many of these magazines, including *Barron's Online*, also can be accessed on the Internet for a fee. We also recommend the *Sound Mind Investing* newsletter and book of the same name. See www.soundmindinvesting.com. Crown Financial Ministries offers this as information and not as an endorsement.

The Christian Financial Planning Institute is an independent, nonprofit organization that provides comprehensive financial advice from highly qualified professionals. For more information visit their Web site, www.christianfpi.org.

Larry Burkett's *Investing for the Future* and mutual fund adviser Austin Pryor's *Sound Mind Investing* are two user-friendly tools, worded in everyday language and presented in easy-to-digest portions. Go to Crown's Web site at ww.crown.org for more investing information.

PERCENTAGE GUIDE FOR FAMILY INCOME
Family of Four
(The Net Spendable percentages also are applicable to Head of Household family of three.)

Gross Household Income	$25,000 or less	$35,000	$45,000	$55,000	$65,000	$85,000	$115,000
1. Tithe	10%	10%	10%	10%	10%	10%	10%
2. Tax	5.1%	14.9%	17.9%	19.9%	21.8%	25.8%	28.1%
Net Spendable Income	$21,225	$26,285	$32,445	$38,555	$44,330	$54,570	$71,185
Net Spendable Income percentages below total 100%							
3. Housing	38%	36%	32%	30%	30%	30%	29%
4. Food	14%	12%	13%	12%	11%	11%	11%
5. Auto	14%	12%	13%	14%	14%	13%	13%
6. Insurance	5%	5%	5%	5%	5%	5%	5%
7. Debts	5%	5%	5%	5%	5%	5%	5%
8. Enter./Recreation	4%	6%	6%	7%	7%	7%	8%
9. Clothing	5%	5%	5%	6%	6%	7%	7%
10. Savings	5%	5%	5%	5%	5%	5%	5%
11. Medical	5%	4%	4%	4%	4%	4%	4%
12. Miscellaneous	5%	5%	7%	7%	8%	8%	8%
13. Investments[1]	—	5%	5%	5%	5%	5%	5%
If you have this expense below, the percentage shown must be deducted from other budget categories.							
14. School/Child Care[2]	8%	6%	5%	5%	5%	5%	5%
15. Unallocated Surplus Income[3]	—	—	—	—	—	—	—

1. This category is used for long-term investment planning, such as caring for elderly parents or retirement.
2. This category is added as a guide only. If you have this expense, the percentage shown must be deducted from other budget categories.
3. This category is used when surplus income is received.

SAVINGS ACCOUNT ALLOCATIONS

Date	Deposit	With-drawal	Balance	Housing	Food	Auto Insur.	Auto Maint.	Insur-ance	Clothing	Medical	Debts				

ACKNOWLEDGMENTS

I would like to sincerely thank my editor, Adeline Griffith, for her time and talents devoted to this and to many other projects.

And I would be remiss if I didn't thank Harvey Nowland for his help in developing the Additional Resources for this book and for his writing expertise.

Many thanks to you both.

Larry Burkett

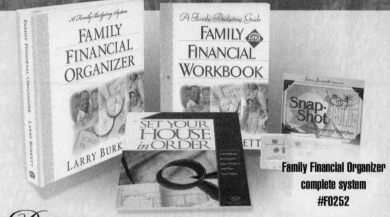

ABOUT THE AUTHOR

Larry Burkett was the founder and president of Christian Financial Concepts (CFC), a nonprofit organization dedicated to teaching principles of money management. In 2000 CFC merged with Crown Ministries (an organization that utilizes small-group studies in churches to provide practical, biblical training in financial stewardship) to form Crown Financial Ministries, of which Larry is Chairman of the Board. He is the bestselling author of more than seventy books, including *Business by the Book, The Coming Economic Earthquake, Your Finances in Changing Times, Investing for the Future,* and *The Illuminati.* He and his wife Judy reside in Georgia and have four grown children and nine grandchildren.

CROWN FINANCIAL MINISTRIES WANTS TO help you become financially free so you'll be able to know Christ more intimately and be free to serve Him. Crown has an extensive range of resources, including volunteer budget counselors, seminars, small-group Bible studies, software, and books. To aid you in your educational and occupational decision making, we have an assessment tool that profiles personality, interests, skills, and work values.

You may contact Crown Financial Ministries through our Web site, www.crown.org; by telephone, (800) 722-1976, or write to us at 601 Broad St. SE, Gainesville, GA 30501-3790.